MW01679410

TESTIMONIALS

"Edwin is the rarest of all business strategists and personal development advisors – he has unique methods that massively increase your performance in all areas of your life both professionally & personally. Edwin is a true master - I should know - he mentors me."

Darren J. Stephens - Melbourne Australia
#1 International Bestselling Author
"Millionaires & Billionaires Secrets Revealed"

"I wanted to take a moment to express my sincere thanks for your participation in our Mastery program. You added so much knowledge, value and fun. I've heard so many comments on how great the mornings' sessions were, and how much the group enjoyed learning about their voices, their bodies and singing. The difference between the group's sound the first morning and the last was incredible! Your flexibility was also very much appreciated. I knew I could count on you to be there the entire time and on time regardless of last minute changes. Your professionalism is inspirational!"

With Love and Respect, Anthony Robbins, Chairman, Robbins Research International, May 1992, USA

"I have never experienced anything so deeply profound and personal as the work Edwin is doing... Communicating from your soul through music has the power to change the world!"

Rita B, USA

"I have been on training courses with some of the leaders in personal development including Tony Robbins, Richard Bandler, Deepak Chopra, Paul McKenna, Wayne Dyer and others - I would rate this course as one of the most enlightening and outstanding I've been on."

Sean K, Ireland

"This experience took me on a journey through creative passages I had never explored, not believed existed - as well as emotional revelations that now have found their home inside me. Even I do not know the full benefits of this experience as they unfold in the days and weeks to come. All I can say is that it was the most awesome experience of my life!"

Marianna C, USA

"I waited a couple of weeks to write a testimonial because I felt that I had experienced shifts that were profound. I wanted to know how alive they were after the initial "high" of the experience passed. I have been attending many personal growth programs for over 26 years. All of them are wonderful, and with most, I have had experiences that are more of a subtle awareness shift. YOUR PROGRAM is different. It lasted! The results have stayed."

Susan A, USA

"The work that Edwin does is clearly universes above what anyone else is doing in this arena. Edwin Coppard is more than a Master voice coach. It's like he reaches into your soul and calls forth your soul's true voice. This is the first time in my life that I experienced what it's like to be really heard."

Daniel D, Canada

"As one of Vancouver's leading session singers (I do over 100 sessions per year, including jingles, album cuts, etc., along with weekly live performances), I found that since I have adopted Edwin's vocal techniques, I haven't had any vocal problems and I have found that vocal eases and warm-ups have especially helped in opening up my voice. I have also found that my range has been very consistent. I would definitely recommend Edwin's method for good vocal strength and durability."

Marc Lafrance, Canada

"Under the expert tuition of Edwin Coppard my daughter and I learned how to unlock the beautiful sound that resides within all of us. The journey took us through an amazing world of archetypes that lie within us all. We spent many days on the secluded beach discovering new territory, previously hidden from our own view. It was exhilarating and liberating and amazing fun."

Bernie OR, UK

"Suffice it to say that what Edwin does goes far beyond what any other voice 'trainer'. His gift is to be able to hear your real sound and call it forth by using tools that align your whole self, thereby freeing your voice so that you can sing in a completely natural way.

I felt that I grew up into my mature feminine right before my very eyes. What amazed me was the effortless grace that came into my voice. Through this program I have been finally able to tap into my own sound, one that has been seeking expressing all my life."

Pamela F, Canada

WAKE UP & SING!

How to unleash the power of your voice

GLOBAL PUBLISHING GROUP

Global Publishing Group
Australia • New Zealand • Singapore • America • London

WAKE UP & SING!

How to unleash the power of your voice

Edwin & Cheryl Coppard

DISCLAIMER

All the information, techniques, skills and concepts contained within this publication are of the nature of general comment only and are not in any way recommended as individual advice. The intent is to offer a variety of information to provide a wider range of choices now and in the future, recognising that we all have widely diverse circumstances and viewpoints. Should any reader choose to make use of the information contained herein, this is their decision, and the contributors (and their companies), authors and publishers do not assume any responsibilities whatsoever under any condition or circumstances. It is recommended that the reader obtain their own independent advice.

First Edition 2012

National Library of Australia
Cataloguing-in-Publication entry:

Coppard, Edwin.
Wake up & sing : how to unleash the power of your voice / Edwin Coppard ; Cheryl Coppard.

1st ed.
ISBN: 9781922118080 (pbk.)

Singing--Instruction and study.
Singing--Studies and exercises.

Other Authors/Contributors: Coppard, Cheryl.

783.043

Published by Global Publishing Group
PO Box 517 Mt Evelyn, Victoria 3796 Australia
Email info@TheGlobalPublishingGroup.com

For Further information about orders:
Phone: +61 3 9736 1156 or Fax +61 3 8648 6871

We dedicate this book to the global reawakening of the full integrity of the human spirit.We dedicate this book to the healing power of song and sound.We dedicate this book to the wild voice in everyone. We dedicate this book to those with the courage, curiosity and humour to voyage inside their uncharted territories.
We dedicate this book to those whose voices and songs have yet to be heard.
We dedicate this book to the spirit of exploration, the magic of the journey.

We were born to express the song of life, the song of the universe, through the marvelous machinery of the body / mind. To sing, to resonate with the swelling undulations of creation – what better way to say "I WAS HERE!"

Edwin and Cheryl Coppard

ACKNOWLEDGEMENTS

We would like to offer a special thanks to those who helped to make this book a reality:

All the people, young and old, from all walks of life, who have come out to our sessions and events over the last many years: your experiences and feedback continue to shape our course!

All those who contributed their songs and stories to this book; thanks for your courage in sharing your deeply personal experiences!

Heartfelt thanks to Miwa Kashu, the heart and soul of Real People Music in Japan: it was your insistence that fueled this project from start to finish. Yes, it did take much longer than anticipated! Your integrity, passion, dedication and mischievousness are a constant inspiration to us!

Thanks to Anthony Robbins for believing in the power of music and in us.

Thanks to James Skinner for your continuing friendship and generosity of spirit.

Thanks to Darren Stephens for believing in us, encouraging us, and guiding us in this book writing adventure. You make it seem easy!

Heartfelt gratitude to Trudy Buckler-Blake, a lighthouse in the dark, and the beginning of our incredible journey.

Deep appreciation to Robert Moore and Douglas Gillette, authors of 'King, Warrior, Magician, Lover: Rediscovering the Archetypes of the Masculine Psyche': their brilliant work was the beginning and foundation of our journey into the inner world of the Living Archetypes.

Thanks to Jill Chivers for your help transposing and helping to organize the first bare bones.

Thanks to Arlaine Johansen for your support whenever, whatever, and wherever.

Deep gratitude to our parents, Edward Coppard and Alice Coppard, and also Roy Johansen and Doreen Johansen for encouraging us and supporting the music inside us. Words can never adequately express the sacredness, power and complexity of the part our parents still play in who we've become.

Thanks to our sons, Ulysses and Zane, passionate musicians, for being themselves.

Last but not least, profound gratitude to Maharishi Mahesh Yogi for teaching us how to experience pure silence within, the basis for all sound.

FREE BONUS GIFT

DVD Valued at $197 – But Yours FREE!

Claim your FREE BONUS GIFTS by going to
ww.RealPeopleMusic.com/Book-Bonus

Instant Access and FREE Download

On this DVD you'll Discover:

- How to fill a room with your energy so that your voice naturally carries and your presence is felt by everyone
- Special breathing technique that will increase your energy and bring a smooth effortless support to your voice
- How to focus your content for maximum impact
- How to conquer fear of the audience

Claim your FREE DVD NOW by going to
ww.RealPeopleMusic.com/Book-Bonus

TABLE OF CONTENTS

"Music gives a soul to the universe, wings to the mind, flight to the imagination, and life to everything."

Plato, Ancient Greek Philosopher
428 BC-348 BC

INTRODUCTION

We've lost our voices and our songs. . So…Wake Up and Sing!

Sing with your Unbounded Voice!

Our modern heart and soul has no voice! Only the mind gets to speak. The mind speaks what is clever / polite / correct / useful / scientifically provable / intelligent / profitable/ acceptable/ socially and politically advantageous. This is the way of all educated societies. But we have 'The Arts' and the megastars, don't we? That rarefied and magical atmosphere where the truly gifted, eccentric, talented, charismatic, fearless and lucky people can express everything so much more perfectly than we ourselves can.

And if we can't afford to see them we can always buy the CD or download their MP3s. We hurry, unheeding, past the lone virtuoso playing Bach in the subway. We hurry by the street musicians, not wanting to part with any change. Instead, we sit back and listen to the radio, the TV, our computer, a full iPod. Plugged into something all day long, we become connoisseurs and critical observers of modern culture while daydreaming about what it would be like for us to command that kind of energy and recognition. And then, when we finally die, we'll die unexpressed, our stories and voices lost, with a rusty soul.

We think there's definitely something wrong with this picture!

When you sing, you simultaneously express all the layers of who you are. Your voice is like your fingerprint and none are alike. The same goes for the stories of your life you carry within you. Nobody else has lived your life. Therefore the sound of your voice and the stories of your songs are unique among the billions of people of the world.

In travelling to many places, all over the world, we have affirmed that most people are not singing anymore. People don't sing on a daily basis. People don't sing together as a matter of course. Some people sing once a week in church, some occasionally sing along to the radio in their car, or some may whistle or sing in the shower, but on the whole it is not very common to hear people singing while you walk around in any city or town.

How did it happen that people stopped singing? In the West it likely began long, long ago, perhaps with the advent of written musical notation. No earlier than the 8th century, the structure of musical notation was beginning to emerge driven by the need of the Catholic Church to establish their chants and liturgies and to transmit them over vast distances. Scholars write about how before the advent of written music, everybody sang. It was only when notes started to be written down that people began to stop singing together, because in that act a deep division was created between people who could read the notes and people who couldn't. People who couldn't read music began to be seen as unmusical, while people who could read it became recognized as musicians. And of course, because only a small segment of society had access to education, most people ended up being 'unmusical'. And out of musical notation came the 'right' frequencies of the notes, the 'right' way to play them, and the 'right' way to sing them.

And working up to modern times, the long arm of Western culture has made its way into every corner of the world, spreading its influence for good and bad. For our purposes, it has unintentionally spread non-singing as the way to live.

During the last hundred years or so, the world has witnessed a cultural backlash against the highly structured framework of Western classical music. Today jazz, rap, and popular music, with their improvisational natures and 'bent' notes, are far more appealing to the mass audiences. Today we are at the opposite end of the spectrum - anything goes! The feeling is one of immense musical freedom, where there can be a market for any kind of musical expression. You can create something today and put it on the internet tomorrow; and, after a few days, half a million people can have heard it!

Why, then, are people still not singing? No matter what other factors are at play, the habit of non-singing begins at home. In your home and in your family. In many previous generations, the governing philosophy was that children should be seen and not heard at home. And when at school, children should sit down, keep still, keep quiet, and not speak unless you're spoken to. So much suppressed expression! This cultural paradigm now seems to be shifting to a more open atmosphere, one more interested in and respectful of who a child really is, and more interested and open to what s/he may have to say than ever before.

Singing is culturally validated, so why are most of us terrified to sing in front of others? Forget public speaking! To sing in front of others brings out far more fear. What if nobody likes my voice? What if I am out of tune? What if I have no rhythm? What if I forget the words? What if I'm not as good as the last person who sang? What if I don't sing perfectly?

Singing in front of others can create huge fear because, while singing, you can't help showing some of the deepest part of yourself. You can't completely hide who you really are. The fear comes because there's always a chance that you won't be received well, that you won't be accepted. Will you be recognized and applauded for who you really are? You may have consciously or unconsciously created a different persona - a way of speaking, a way of walking, a way of dressing, or a way of acting that is somewhat contrary to who you are inside. Most of us have, at some time or other. When you sing, it's a lot harder to hide behind the persona you have created. We tend to show something of our true selves when we sing.

The aim of this book is not to teach you how to sing! We want to guide you to discover your Unbounded Voice and bring to life the passion, the stories and the voice inside you that needs and wants to be expressed! We want you to know and experience that singing is natural for everyone, everywhere!

We see ourselves as a force for reawakening the soul's voice! We are also creating a forum for these voices and songs to be heard around the whole world. Through the transformative power of writing and singing our own songs, we can heal our lives and bring blessings to others.

"To stop the flow of music would be like the stopping of time itself, incredible and inconceivable."

Aaron Copland 1900 – 1990
American Composer

Chapter 1

What has Happened to Our Voices?

Chapter 1
What has Happened to Our Voices?

The voices of our hearts and souls have become lost deep inside. The art of being able to effortlessly express ourselves through singing and sound has been lost to popular culture for a long time. We believe that the basic human need for self-expression must be met if we are to be happy in life.

It's become a habit to hold back the expression of our emotions. It's become a habit to express emotion through language alone, through the spoken or the written word.

Emotion can be expressed purely with sound - a baby crying. As we grow, it takes us some years to master speaking and to begin to translate our emotions into words. It is not easy. In essence we take the currents of our feelings inside and attempt to distill them into a few words. We stop the currents of our emotions in the attempt to describe them. We walk over to the other side of our brain to do this, and, in this process, become somewhat detached from what we were feeling in the first place. This is the inherent problem with expressing emotion through language.

Language is very much a manufactured sound. The sounds of language are created with the lips, the mouth, the tongue, the jaw and the throat by modifying the primordial sounds that are naturally created by the body. We modify these raw sounds into the precise codes of language that are so necessary for us. Though always evolving, language is not universal. Even a few kilometers away our language may not be understood by anyone.

It is necessary and natural to speak and to write, but it is an incomplete and sad picture without singing. We need to sing to express the wholeness of our emotions and ourselves.

What has become socially acceptable is expressing the right words but with no emotion. Even though you may perfectly express the words that describe your emotion, it doesn't mean you have expressed the emotion itself. The bulk of the emotional energy remains trapped in your body. The result is something Edwin and I call suppressed expression, and, from what we can see, most countries on Earth are under the influence of mass suppressed expression. We believe it counts for a large percentage of society's ills, from depression and suicide to anti-social behaviour.

Edwin has a personal story that illustrates the power of suppressed expression:

Edwin*: "When I was a young man at boarding school in England, church services were provided weekly. Once a month or so, as a courtesy, the local village priest was invited in to give the service.*

The reverend was a nice fellow, but the word was that he had been deeply traumatized in the war, and as a consequence he had a very pronounced and peculiar mannerism. It would come up when he spoke: he'd start a sentence and then half way through it he would stick out his neck violently and raise his arms as he was finishing the sentence. It really was the most bizarre spectacle.

Put yourself in our positions as 14, 15 and, 16 year old young men. We did not know how to handle this emotionally. Our teachers were dozing in the back of the room pretending nothing was amiss. To us it was like some sort of freak show. At the same time we were not allowed to make noise. We'd get into trouble. The whole school was present there, three hundred to four hundred students, and as the reverend gave his sermon nobody was allowed to make a sound. What happened was that the emotions started to build.

Sooner or later, somebody lost control, perhaps 4 or 5 rows down from you. You'd see him with his body shaking in a kind of silent laughter that he was trying desperately to muffle. Sometimes boys put handkerchiefs into their mouths, and air seemed to be coming out of their ears and their eyes with the desperate attempt to stop the sound. It would creep down the row. You could see it coming towards you, as it went from one person to another person, and this shaking laughter was creeping towards you silently and you knew it was coming. Then suddenly the guy next to you started to shake. Finally, inevitably, you lost control, too. You were just desperately trying to hold it back, while in the back of the room the teachers were pretending to be asleep. Nobody knew how to handle the situation.

At our school we prided ourselves on being really bad singers. We had this attitude that it was not cool to sing well. We made a point of singing gleefully and horribly out of tune. We would sort of groan through the songs - one-note songs in the key of groan. When I think back I realize how it must have been excruciatingly torturous for the music master. But, in this circumstance with the local reverend, the singing became a golden opportunity to actually let out the sounds of suppressed laughter. Suddenly everyone sang at about 20 times the normal volume. When a hymn came up, we were shouting and singing at the top of our lungs, our faces well hidden behind the hymnbooks, with peals of laughter going through the room. It was a completely insane zoo, with the shrieking and singing and laughter, but we got away with it. We were finally allowed to make the sounds that our bodies were desperate to make and express."

It can be incredibly difficult to hold back what you need to express. And when you finally choose to express it, it can seem to come out quite out of control. We've all had the experience of not knowing how to handle something, and holding in our anger, and then when finally we can't hold it in any longer and let it out, it often comes out with an intensity that we regret after the fact.

Perhaps this is another reason why people are afraid of singing, because they feel they may not be able to control the old bottled up emotions coming up. We've seen again and again that when these emotions are naturally released in the context of song and sound, what was perhaps deeply painful and even traumatizing becomes beautiful, profound and healing for all who hear it.

And even if we are someone who loves to sing, and wants to expand our singing potential, we are faced with the fear of social censure. Clients regularly say that they are extremely embarrassed to do the singing workout at home because of how people might think about them and the wild sounds that may be coming from their apartments. Edwin asks them, 'What is better, that people think you are crazy or that you actually become crazy from holding it all inside?'

People may be more open than we think:

Edwin: *"I was on the beach early one morning in Tofino, Canada. I was just making some sound, and suddenly this very strong wave of energy came up in my body. I can't exactly remember what I did but it was loud and wild. After a while the sound settled down and I noticed some people walking on the beach. My first thought was, 'They must think I am crazy, they must think I am nuts.' I could not avoid walking past them as I left the beach. As I walked by, one of them said, "Was that you making that sound?" I mumbled, "Yes." "Wow, those sounds you were making, they were amazing," they replied."*

You might not get that reaction. Truthfully it is none of anyone else's business, except possibly if you are expressing your full voice in the middle of the night when they are trying to sleep! If they have a problem it is usually their own. If they complain we suggest that rather than be on the apologetic defensive, explain it to them, educate them. Here is your chance to tell them about this new thing you have discovered, and that when you make these sounds it feels so good.

Here's another story about social attitudes and 'unacceptable' sounds:

Edwin: *"In my young musician days I lived with a nurse in a house that had been converted into five small apartments with very thin walls. One of the other tenants was an architect who worked at home. I had musician's hours and was often at home during the day as well. The architect's girlfriend often came to visit him during the day. They would make love and she would sing at the top of her lungs. It sounded like opera. What do you do? The other tenants in the house used to join in on the sounds just for fun. One day a friend came to visit one of the tenants and was interrupted by the sounds. All the tenants were quite used to the sounds by now, but his shocked guest made a loud and insulting remark. The couple on the other side of the wall went quiet for about a minute and then resumed where they left off, outrageously and joyfully unconcerned about the opinions of others. I have to say I admired their attitude."*

The effect of criticism on our voices is definitely an area that has to be addressed. We have heard thousands of stories about how someone's voice was crushed by criticism. One nun told a woman that she had the worst voice she had ever heard. What a thing to say to anybody! We've heard enough stories of how children in elementary school were told to mouth the words instead of singing them that it seems this was a quite a common practice. Another, a schoolteacher, taped the child's mouth shut with masking tape because he wouldn't stop talking. People laughed and made fun of him afterwards as well. Not surprisingly, even thirty years or so later, or so when he gets in front of an audience and starts to speak, he begins to sweat profusely. His body holds the memory of being publicly censured, humiliated and helpless, not even being able to open his mouth. This boy had just needed to be heard somehow. To be received and to be understood and perhaps guided with some boundaries if his behaviour was totally unacceptable. This happens to so many people when they sing or when they express themselves freely in their natural energy; they get subdued or criticized or ridiculed in some very cruel ways. So most of us get the message that it is not necessarily safe to show who we really are. Most of us decide to just fit in and not be anything. That kills us. That kills us inside. We become robotic, we become unsatisfied, unexpressed, unfulfilled in so many ways.

So many people have shut down and just stopped singing. Some of the worst culprits are singing teachers and choir directors telling people, even children at an early age, 'No, you can't sing in tune; no, you can't be in the choir,' instead of helping them find their voices and their natural ability to sing.

"Music is the essence of order" **- Plato**

It is a law of nature that music creates order out of chaos. Plato said, "Music is the essence of order". That is the truth of it, and if a person is allowed and encouraged to experience and experiment in finding their voice, then the order Plato spoke of will be quickly created inside. In every case a strong, natural, consistent and beautiful voice will quickly emerge. A voice that can sing anything we want it to sing, naturally and powerfully. We tolerate people experimenting with instruments, and you know it is often not too pleasant to listen to; some guy squealing on the bagpipes trying how to figure out how to find the right notes, somebody squawking away scales on a clarinet, or a trumpet so loud and badly off key. We don't seem to mind too much because we all know that in order to become proficient at anything, mistakes will be made in the beginning, maybe even for years. Yet we seldom extend that courtesy to our own voices or the voices of others. It doesn't seem to be acceptable to be heard making even a few 'mistakes' when we open our mouths in song.

Singing teachers. Where to begin? We believe that the teaching of singing has really gotten off track. A lot of singing technique has become the quest for total control of the voice rather than real freedom with the natural voice. When we are born the voice is fully connected to the body in sound. As we learn to speak the voice becomes more and more connected to the mind. Modern voice training and classical voice training treats singing as a language using the mind and hearing to control the voice. We feel that this is a primary misunderstanding of the universal principles of sound and singing.

The idea and practice of attempting to completely control the voice in the name of singing perfectly correct notes and having perfectly correct tone has gone wildly astray. In the long run, this has resulted in subverting the simple, natural joy of everyone singing, and singing together.

Cheryl: *"I remember hearing a highly trained singer for the first time as a young child, and I remember running out of the room to get away from the sound."*

Think about it –what music, what kind of tones and/or sound production would make someone, however small, react by running away from it?

Music is supposed to lift you up inside. It's supposed to bring beauty and harmony into your soul and bring people together in appreciation. It's true that profound beauty can be found in classical vocal music, but we feel that the music has become a slave to our strange obsession to try and force our voices into a mental ideal of perfect control. Of course there are always exceptions, those who can sing freely no matter what the genre, but they seem to be the exception rather than the rule.

Our bottom line is that the free sounds we make as a child are meant to naturally evolve into our fully connected adult singing voice. Our voice is by far the best musical instrument on earth in terms of its range of tone and infinite ability to express and communicate anything! And when our emotions are naturally expressed through singing, the energy and flow of our life force is released, like a tap being turned on. Thus our health and wellbeing are kept at the highest level. Singing is the easiest and most graceful way to express the wholeness of who we are. It is a glorious gift of nature and sadly underused by most of us.

We also wonder why singing is not employed more as a learning tool in school. Think back; we'll bet that you can still remember at least one song you learned in elementary school. Can you say the same thing for what you may have learned in University?

Cheryl: *"While in high school over 30 years ago, I had a very eccentric French teacher who centred his lessons around songs he taught us to sing. His crude accompaniment on his battered, perennially out-of-tune guitar seemed more about entertainment than learning. However, to this day I remember several of the songs he taught, though the rest of my French is definitely in tatters. Thank you, Dr. Gallagher!"*

Our cultural educational focus seems to go primarily into learning how to read and write - in our opinion too early. In most school systems, the body's wisdom and the body's needs are neglected more and more each year as we advance in grade. Because of this, and also because no one else around us seems to be singing, we stop the natural evolution of our voice into a perfect and powerful singing instrument. But because everyone around us is also doing it, we don't realize what we are losing until we wake up one day as an adult feeling hollow and disconnected. Most of us have a huge weight of suppressed expression and no idea how we got to that place.

How about considering: What has happened to your voice? Do you sing? Do you remember any feedback regarding your voice? When did you stop singing and why?

"The singer has everything within him. The notes come out from his very life. They are not materials gathered from outside."

Rabindranath Tagore, Indian Poet, playwright and essayist, 1861 – 1941

Chapter 2

What Is Our Natural Voice?

Chapter 2

What Is Our Natural Voice?

So here's the big question: what IS our natural voice?

We are born with a full natural voice, and, if we observe babies and young children, we can learn a lot about it. Tiny little babies can express a tremendous amount of sound, often louder than the adults around them. They never go hoarse, even after prolonged crying bouts. Most adults would be hoarse within ten minutes of attempting to release the same intensity of sound. The simple reason for this is babies are in a 'body' voice and adults tend to be in a 'mind' voice. We learn the 'mind' voice when we learn to speak by attempting to imitate the sounds around us. We listen and we copy, and this process of learning puts us in the mind and takes us away from the free sounds of the body. As time passes and this process evolves, we become more embedded in the mind as we try to understand everything that is being said around us.

Babies, with the range of tone within their sound, can get everything they need without speaking a single word! It is such a simple, natural thing and a mother soon learns the vocabulary of her baby's sounds. Sometimes just making the sound alone is enough to satisfy a discontented child. The baby and the pre-language child spontaneously create sound to express themselves and get their needs met. They're not thinking, "If I can only control my diaphragm properly I'll be able to project my voice across the room to where my mother is".

The reason children are so free with their sound and voice, and we are not, is because they are so free, active and flexible in their bodies and emotions. When a baby cries, he cries with his whole body, his whole being. That is why it is so loud and so compelling. A child has such emotional flexibility - all parents marvel at the way their child's emotions can turn on a dime. One moment they are crying as if the world is ending, and in the blink of an eye they'll be laughing and playing, tears forgotten. Little kids have so much energy in their bodies, too. They're always moving. They can drive us wonderfully crazy because they never stop. They run rings around us all day long and never seem to get that physical exhaustion that we do. Their bodies are free and relaxed, and their emotional response is unfettered.

This idyllic state of affairs generally starts to come to an end around the age of two when we stop making these raw, primal sounds and focus on speaking instead. Perhaps we also learn to be seen and not heard. And then when we go to school most of us learned to sit down, be still, and speak only with permission. And of course get the right answer.

Naturally, some order must be created in the classroom, but we find it shocking and disturbing to see the statistics on how much we are now medicating our children in order to keep them still. There must be a better way! We believe a program of sound, singing, movement, song writing and self -expression should be essential education for every child through all grades. It will teach them how to be effortlessly creative, to express their individuality, to build their identities, and to have the stories of their lives heard through their songs. In so doing, they will also learn to listen to others as they would like to be listened to. They would be creating a foundation for self-expression for the rest of their lives. Think of what that could have been like when we went to school!

The process of education in the westernized cultures seems to take us further and further away from the spontaneous physical and emotional freedoms we enjoyed as children. During the years of education, we all seem to migrate further and further into our heads, until all that is natural is educated right out of us, and, as adults, we must work to discover it all over again if we want to feel alive. There is an over emphasis on learning to read, write, memorize and compute. There is not enough emphasis on learning how to stay happy, healthy and creative our whole lives.

Our natural adult singing voice evolves from our child's preverbal voice. With the proper guidance and encouragement and without negative criticism, those free, loud sounds so seemingly out of tune are destined to evolve into a beautiful and natural singing voice.

As a society, if we could only encourage the development of the natural singing voice, from a very young age, this singing voice would allow us the full expression of our emotions for the rest of our lives.

It is completely natural to sing. Singing is not a trained experience. We humans are made to sing; because only in physically singing can we express and enliven all the tones of our body and energies of our emotions. In other words, we need to sing to remain healthy physically, emotionally and spiritually. The natural voice emerges from that child sound and evolves into the tones and musical shapes that become our music.

Another important consideration: in the pursuit of our natural voice, we must honour our biology if we want to develop our fullest vocal potential. Are we a male or are we a female? Logically, if we try and sing like a woman and we are a man the result will be strain and possibly long lasting damage to our voice.

And vice versa. It's ironic then that when listening to popular music on the radio, it can be very difficult to tell if a man or a woman is singing. The men tend to be singing very high, splitting their voices and singing falsetto and the women tend to be singing primarily in what is called the 'chest' voice and singing very low. Both these styles of singing could be said to be using techniques of force and ultimately they cause a strain on the physiology and can damage the instrument itself over time. These days it is rare to hear the thrilling and resonant tones of a mature masculine voice or the pure soaring free female voice in any style. It's become the exception rather than the rule.

Edwin: *"I want to mention the only important singing teacher I had, and what she said to me when I decided to teach voice lessons. Her name was Trudy Buckler-Blake. When I told her about my decision to teach she told me not to teach women to sing like men. She said that there is a fundamental difference in the male and female voice, but that men had been teaching women to sing like men. Essentially and simply, women access the feminine resonance when they sing high and men connect with pure masculine energy in the low notes. Every man can sing to the bottom note on the piano, and every woman can vocalize higher than most people imagine. We have socialized our voices into a mid range muddle of homogenized sexuality."*

We don't have the intention to limit the range of anyone's voice - quite the opposite, but for us it is essential that the basic masculine and feminine qualities of sound and resonance are established first and foremost.

The biggest mistake we make as adults wanting to sing has been to go back to our educational model, to go into our minds and try and make our voice come out perfect. Disaster! Instead of going into our heads, we need experiential learning. We need to go through a similar process of learning that every child, every person, goes through when they learn anything physical - from baking cookies to riding a bike; that is, we must connect and coordinate the body with the mind. Singing is like anything else you learn; at first there'll be many different kinds of 'mistakes' - sounds out of context, incomplete sound sequences, inability to make certain sounds, etc. In the process of rediscovering your voice you will likely make many musical mistakes. So what! The mistakes become part of the fun, part of the process, part of the surprise of it all. They become the marker for you to see how far you've come.

The act of singing is an event of coordination between the mind, body and emotions. How well we sing depends upon the degree of coordination. We need to get our body involved. We need to get our body energy involved.

When people think of the art of singing, their thoughts often go to trained or classical singers, the singers of Musical Theatre, Opera, and Lieder. These singers are held up as the pinnacles of human vocal achievement by most cultured people. They are considered to be the only 'real' singers.

We disagree. In general we feel that this kind of training has become technical in a way that the technique gets in the way of the natural production of sound. To put it another way, technique is not the way that we sing. There is no great singer, great artist, or highly accomplished person in any field that ever describes his or her greatest moment or highest achievement in terms of technique. A friend of Edwin's knows a singer who was going to perform with Luciano Pavarotti, one of opera's greats who has now passed on. She was very nervous when she went to rehearse with him. She went over to his house and was shocked when he said something like, 'Oh, rehearsal. Forget about it. Let's just have some tea and chat. Surely you know the music by now.' Part of his genius was that he knew that too much focus on technique and trying to 'make it perfect' kills the music.

Many people have the idea that they can sing only by using the right technique.

The word 'technique' in singing has come to mean the closely guarded secrets of specific manipulations of the body and breath, jaw and mouth to create the manufactured sounds that are in line with a particular style. Most of these singing techniques override the natural system in such a way that the natural sound is adulterated, stifled, changed, lost and even damaged. Singing in this way means that music comes from outside ourselves, as we try and imitate what the teacher has asked for. And this disconnects us from the inherent ability of our bodies to create perfect sound and music. We lose the very point of what singing is about, which is to allow the body to create the sounds and melodies it needs to bring itself into balance while telling our stories.

Pele, the great soccer player, in an attempt to describe his almost supernatural ability to go around many players at once said, "I go through them!" He never talked about techniques of fancy footwork, strategy, conditioning, or breathing. Roger Bannister described religious experiences when he broke the world record and won his race with the first four-minute mile. He didn't mention techniques of stride, strategy or breathing either.

From their descriptions of the events, these men were all in 'the zone' at the time of their great accomplishments. We would define being in 'the zone' as a time of the nearly perfect coordination of our inner resources. While in 'the zone' we seem to magically exceed the limits of our current potential. Anybody can go into 'the zone' at any time, and many people experience it regularly, those times when everything seems to flow effortlessly, joyfully and with great energy and clarity. It is a place of surprising simplicity and calm. The way we would describe it is that it feels like we're riding a glorious cosmic wave and can't fall off. We believe that exceptional people tend to live in 'the zone' most of the time.

This 'zone' state is far too complex to create with our minds or any kind of singing technique. 'The zone' is absolutely where we want to be when we sing. But we don't try to achieve it by using difficult and/or isolating techniques to manipulate, control and force the voice, breathing or any part of our body. We create it by setting the stage; in other words, we want to reset the conditions of the body / mind / emotions with simple exercises that create a state of maximum coordination and maximum flexibility. We want to free the nervous system as much as possible so it can naturally respond in the appropriate way to the demands of a song and the setting - the phrasing, tonality and emotion, all within the context of a certain size room for a certain audience or recording. It is impossible to calculate and address in the mind all these variables to create the greatest outcome. We let the inner intelligence of our bodies do it for us.

We find that when people are in 'the zone', more than 90 percent of musicality and sound production are taken care of. It seems magical. Edwin rarely uses technical advice or even musical language when teaching a song or piece of music.

Here's a poignant example:

Edwin: *"A group of four women asked me to coach them with a song that they were due to perform. They were in a panic trying to remember the music, the words, the harmonies, and the piano accompanist was making mistakes as well. They had been working on the song for over a month. I felt they must know it well by now, but there was something else going on. I could have checked all the musical parameters such as notes, rhythm, pitch and such, but instead I asked them what the song was about. It turned out that the song was called "I Want To Be An Old Woman" and they were all women in their 50s. They'd chosen the song as an empowerment exercise. I asked them what they thought about becoming old. One woman replied that she just thought of her mother who was old, miserable and dying. It went downhill from there. In the forthcoming discussion I found that everyone's view of old age was really dark, not only concerning people they knew but also the general condition of the elderly in our society. These women seemed to have nothing to look forward to.*

I set about going deeper into their references to old age. Finding out for each of them what the song really meant. Not just their mental conditioning but also their body experience. We discovered that old age was empowering on so many levels. It embodied wisdom, freedom, family, grandchildren, spiritual fulfillment, and so much more. An amazing thing happened when they sang the song again. It was a close to a perfect performance. It was in tune, harmonious, and had beautiful tone. It was so emotionally moving to be in the presence of four women celebrating the power of their maturity that it caused tears to flow down my face.

Case closed. I did not correct their musicality in any way; I knew that they knew the song. All their musical problems had their basis in a lack of connection with the true value of the song."

Singing techniques are overrated. A great technique - what we would call a 'process' because it implies a mind/body experience - puts you in 'the zone' so that the body's own intelligence wakes up and functions perfectly to produce the desired result with ease and excellence. Technique is not how we sing! In fact, Edwin finds himself having to come up with processes to undo the conditioning of people who have trained in too much technique, because it gets in the way of the natural voice.

Instead of trying to use many techniques to cobble together some semblance of what somebody else thinks we should sound like, why don't we free our natural voice instead?

How about: starting to move your body any way it wants, and at the same time spontaneously making sound any way it wants to come out. You can do this in any position: standing, sitting, or lying down. Do it for as long as you want to!

"To be yourself in a world that is constantly trying to make you something else is the greatest accomplishment."

Ralph Waldo Emerson, American poet,
Lecturer and essayist 1803 - 1882

Chapter 3

Our Unique Approach to Singing

Chapter 3

Our Unique Approach to Singing

We don't teach people how to sing in terms of a technical method of breath control or tone control. We don't train people on how to shape the mouth, how to pronounce the words in a certain way, how to place the tone in certain places in the mouth, or how to support the breath from the diaphragm. We do not approach training the voice from the classical paradigm. We don't try to teach singing to people by putting them into the box of any existing model - be it rap, classical, indie, pop, metal; be it bass, baritone, tenor, contralto, alto, or the various types of soprano.

We have found a way to help people unlock the power, beauty, and uniqueness of their natural voice. We have found that the natural voice comes out spontaneously under the right conditions. We have found that when these conditions are met, the voice changes instantly: someone who couldn't sing in tune now magically sings in tune; someone who could only sing a few sequential notes magically gains an octave; a woman who couldn't sing high notes magically can, and a man who couldn't sing low notes magically can; someone who doesn't seem to have a sense of timing now magically has rhythm, and so on. The key is in helping the mind and body reconnect and thus regain the flexibility of childhood, which is not as difficult as it sounds. Essentially it is simple.

Edwin: *"While at Tony Robbins' Life Mastery course in Maui, a woman volunteered for a demonstration on stage. I had her vocal ease with my piano and she sang to the 'C' above middle 'C'. After that, it became strained and difficult for her to go any higher. I muscle tested her to see what part of her body was disconnected from her voice. The hip area came up. I had her sit on the floor with her legs apart and move back and forth from the hips while singing. She sang to a 'G' above middle 'C' - a 5-note increase. Then she broke down in tears. I asked her what she was feeling. She said: '"Anger".' I wasn't certain that this was accurate, so I asked her where she felt the anger. She said she couldn't feel it. I asked her, "Where do you feel anything?' and she pointed to her inner thighs. I asked her what she felt there. She said, "Fear".' That felt congruent. I asked her to move and sing again, riding the wave of fear. Oh, my God! She sang to a 'G', an octave (8 notes) higher than previously with such openness and energy the whole room lit up. The audience of 3,000+ stood up and went crazy on the energy. It turned out that she had been sexually abused in her family, and that was the energy that was trapped in her body and disconnected from her voice. She stood up and jumped around with pure joy for several minutes, she was so energized! Not only did she get her female voice back, she had healed on a profound level."*

In fact, we don't really teach people to sing! It would be like trying to teach people to sleep. Everybody already knows how to sleep and what the experience of sleeping feels like. It's part of being human, though many people may have difficulty sleeping through the night. It's the same with singing. It's deeply hardwired into us, though our voices may not obey us on command.

We feel that when you try to sing by controlling the body and the breath, you stop your own natural flow and you don't allow yourself to tap into the tremendous energy of what is already going on inside. Rather you try to stop it and change it, thinking you know better than Mother Nature, better than the innate intelligence of your own body!

Rather, we observe the natural phenomena of how singing evolves from the original sounds of childhood. The child makes expressive sounds spontaneously, and these sounds are the basis for the development of both language and singing. Speaking and singing are both learned skills, honed by years of constant repetition until, as an adult, we have become an expert in expressing ourselves through language and song. This is the natural way the voice unfolds. In other words, our environment is key in the development of our singing ability. If people are singing around us as often as people are speaking around us we will naturally develop into good singers. If you've gone to small villages in Africa and Fiji, as Edwin has, you will be amazed to see how everyone sings there, and how beautifully they all sing together. Interestingly, there are no singing teachers there.

Let's put this in another prospective. Singing starts from the natural evolution of the wild sounds of a child. As a pre-verbal child, we express ourselves freely on the whole. We make sound to express whatever we are feeling. We move freely also. But from about the age of two on we are conditioned to control our emotions and our physical movements. We learn to speak and then to read and write. Over time, without the naturally balancing experience of singing, there is an over-emphasis on intellectual development alone that further disconnects us from our emotions and can isolate us in our thinking minds for the rest of our lives.

For decades we've watched peoples' natural voices return. For decades we've watched people get back in touch with their authentic emotions. For decades we've watched people get back in touch with and 're-inhabit' their bodies again. Because of this, we are absolutely convinced that we humans are meant to learn to sing along with learning to speak. Definitely before learning to read and write. Why? Because, in essence, this means as you're learning to sing, you're growing in easy and natural body wisdom that will serve you for a lifetime. You're learning to listen to your body and your emotions in a very simple and effective way. This all adds up to incalculable benefits for the health of the body, mind and spirit. We stay healthier physically. We stay healthier creatively. We stay healthier emotionally. We stay healthier spiritually.

Depending upon where we're from, most of us come from generations of non-singers. And that's what most of us would say about ourselves; that we are non-singers. Historically, we live in a culture where people don't sing, and, because of this, children are not getting the proper input to enable them to develop into strong, natural singers. If people were singing around you as you were growing up, you would naturally model them. You would naturally feel that singing was easy and fun. This is the reason many people get a strong urge to sing and must go and seek out a singing teacher. They are trying to replace the experience they missed. Singing is so natural that it doesn't seem right not to be able to sing.

We at Real People Music want to reawaken the singer within everyone around the world! As we have said, though singing is an inherent ability it is a learned skill as well.

Edwin's own learning breakthrough came when he was a professional musician in his 30s.

Edwin: *"One day as I sat at the piano I started wondering, 'How do you sing?' I realized I had no real control over my voice. Some nights my voice would respond brilliantly, and other nights, no matter how much energy I put into it, nothing seemed to be there. I remember just sitting at the piano wondering, 'How do you actually sing?' It was, and I think it still is, a very deep question. I wanted the knowledge of it. I wanted to know what is this phenomenon of singing? I had no idea of where to start, so I looked for an expert, I looked for a teacher."*

This is where Trudy Buckler-Blake came in. She herself was talented and disciplined enough to have won a Ford Foundation Scholarship in New York City. As part of her prize, she studied with the world famous diva Rosa Ponselle who sang with the New York Met for 18 years and was regarded as 'immaculate' by Pavarotti. Trudy was with her for three years or so. After her study was completed and Trudy was preparing to make her public debut - the playbills had already even been printed - she was involved in a tragic car accident. As a result, her vocal cords were damaged and she was told she would never sing again. And for a period of time she didn't. She burned her music and destroyed her recordings.

Some years passed, and she finally decided she needed to see if she could find her voice again. She was married to Dr. Bill Buckler at the time, a physiologist. Together they explored the physical mechanics of what actually happens in our breathing and body when we sing. Her husband would explain and verify physically certain things that she instinctively knew, and she would experiment on herself. Though her voice never returned to its pre-accident strength, she healed her voice and was able to sing again. Her methods were radical. She was completely out of the box. She got wonderful results with people, getting them to go into ranges they would never have even thought possible".

Trudy opened Edwin's eyes to the physical aspect of singing, the simplicity of it, the truth of it, and the necessity of its application and understanding.

The truth is that the whole body breathes and the whole body sings. Remember the baby producing mega decibels from its tiny body, able to go on and on without ever going hoarse? The baby is instinctively using its whole body to breathe, make sound and express emotion. The baby doesn't know how to hold back.

How do they do that, and how can we replicate it in order to have the full power of our sound available to us as adults?

First and foremost, when the baby is crying, its body is instinctively and naturally responding to its needs with perfect efficiency. The baby is operating at an extremely high level of mind/body coordination. This is the way we are born! Even though small babies seem to lie around all day, you don't see them with stiff necks or sore backs! They can fall asleep in the most uncomfortable-looking positions and wake up perfectly refreshed, flexible, and ready to go.

As adults most of us seem to get in a rut physically. We become creatures of habit. We tend to do the same things over and over again, day after day. We might drive to the same job, sit in the same chair, look at the same computer screen, and when we get home we sit on the same couch and wind down watching the same shows on TV. Our physical activities tend to narrow down. Is it any wonder most of us aren't flexible anymore? We're not talking about flexibility solely in terms of actual physical flexibility, but also flexibility in terms of your mind and body being able to respond to any new demand you place on it - a new dance step for example.

Singing is a physical event, so we need to make sure that the whole body is involved. We need to create the circumstances where the energy of the whole body can respond and be connected to the production of sound. We need to regain, or at least improve upon our level of mind/body coordination. No matter what the level of our health or age, there is always room for growth. It's really magical to see how quickly the body can start to move again after years of inactivity and what begins to happen when it does.

One of the strategies we use to help free the natural voice is to use many types of both proven and innovative simple mind/body coordination and left/right brain integration exercises. You get your body moving again in ways that maybe you haven't moved in years! Don't worry, it doesn't hurt, and is easy and enjoyable. The object is not to physically exercise muscles, but to reopen the body's channels of energy and increase coordination. Think of Elvis Presley and the way he was always moving his hips. This is a simple example of the amount of energy that can be expressed if that area of the body is free.

Another strategy we use to bring out the full potential of the natural voice is sound itself. Not music but sound. Again, we want to build on something that was lost in our non-singing culture during childhood when we started to try and channel all our expression into speech alone. Over the years we've lost the fullness, lost the freedom and range of tone. What is tone? It is the unique quality of the sound itself - full or penetrating, light or rich and all the points in between. Your tone is what makes your voice unique and distinguishable from all others. It is like hearing a cello, a trumpet, a piccolo and an accordion all play the note 'A'. None of their sounds would be confused with the other because of the unique tones of the various instruments. The tone of the instrument depends upon the materials and structures that make it up. It is the same with us: our natural tone is created by an integration of the materials (the nature of our cells, the layers of our personality and psyche, our breath) and structures (the dimensions and proportions of our body) that make us ourselves. In order to experience the fulfilment of singing we need to reawaken the tones of our bodies.

How is a pleasing, full tone created in our voice? We look at the whole body as a singing instrument, and this can be explained in a simple way by the way a stereo system works. In a stereo system there is a CD and a mechanism to pick up the sounds from the CD. There is also the amplifier and at least one speaker. In translating this into a human body, the cone in the speaker - the mechanism that focuses the sound - would be the mouth. The magnet in the speaker - the mechanism that creates the sounds - would be the vocal cords. The CD would be the music we have inside us, and our breath would be the mechanism that picks up the musical information from inside and brings it out. The amplifier would be the body itself in its entirety.

If any part of the stereo system or the coordination between its different components is not working, the music will not be heard as intended.

It's the same with the human production of sound. If you are not connected to your own music inside, if your inner CD is misplaced, you cannot possibly express or share that precious part of yourself with anyone. If your breath is jammed and being forced through your throat, the beauty of your voice can be distorted, you can easily go hoarse, and you can have difficulty with rhythm. If the muscles controlling the vocal cords are tight or the vocal cords are damaged in any way, the sound will often be inconsistent or out of tune. If your jaw is rigid, then only a small amount of sound can come out. If the body is stiff and immobile, the sound will lack resonance and dynamics, and can also be out of tune and lack range. Each of these aspects of sound production is important. Equally important is the connection, the coordination between them.

This stereo system analogy also clarifies the distinction between the 'mind' voice and the 'body' voice. In creating the 'mind' voice, the mind tries to tell the voice what to do. The mind tells the vocal cords what sound to make to create the sounds it thinks it wants - to be musically perfect, to please the audience, to imitate someone else, or to please the teacher. It's like the CD going straight to the speaker, bypassing the amplifier. The pure and natural resonance of the body sound is missed. Not to mention the energetic support that the body gives the voice to make singing effortless. The 'body' voice is created by the connection of the voice with the body energy spontaneously responding to create the perfect sound at every moment, like in a child. The CD goes through the amplifier and then to the speaker for optimal sound quality.

In order to experience and express the full potential of your voice, all parts of your stereo system must be functioning and working together. There must be coordination between your music, your breath, your vocal cords, your jaw and mouth area, and your entire body. Every step we take in the direction of freeing the body and increasing coordination between the different aspects of our sound production will give us improvements in the tone, quality, consistency, and range of sound we can produce.

Our entire body is a resonating chamber and every sound we make vibrates through it, evoking emotion, bringing memory, health and healing, coordination and strength. We use only a small percentage of these tones in speaking, and our bodies and our beings are crying out to experience our full range. Most of us have forgotten about these sounds and how good they make us feel, both to make them and to listen to them.

Key to our approach is awakening the connection of sound and singing in the body. It is the connection of your voice in your body. Our teaching protocols are designed to bring you back to that place where the sound flows freely, naturally, and fully. This doesn't necessarily mean that the sound comes out quiet, melodious, sweet and perfect. It might be wild, loud and raw! Everybody's different!

What we've found is that when the natural voice is awakened, it is always beautiful. Everyone's voice has a unique and powerful beauty.

Edwin: *"I had been working with my teacher Trudy for a couple of years, and many changes had occurred in my singing and my voice. One day she read me an article about a Seattle voice teacher who said that if Enrico Caruso (a famous opera singer who died in 1921) opened his voice fully in a small room, it would sound gross. He went on to say that most singing teachers make the mistake of making the students sound nice in the room, and that most people make the same mistake of trying to sound nice in their own heads. Something happened to me when I heard that, and when I sang again I could not hear my voice, there was just pure energy coming through me. When I heard the tape played back, I hardly recognized my voice. I was singing beautiful Opera, something I had never done. I had no idea I had it in me, and it made me cry. My body was ready, through Trudy's training, but my mind had been trying to make me sound nice in my own head."*

How about: experimenting and seeing how body movement affects your voice? We suggest singing 'Row, Row Your Boat' or something equally simple while moving your body. Try several renditions: strong, dynamic movements and then soft, flowing movements. Experiment with many different kinds of movements and just sing. See what happens!

"When I wished
to sing of love, it
turned to sorrow.
And when I wished
to sing of sorrow,
it was transformed
for me into love."

Franz Schubert, Austrian composer
1797-1828

Chapter 4

Riding the Waves of Emotion

Chapter 4

Riding the Waves of Emotion

When we sing we express emotion, no two ways about it; in fact, it could be said that singing is flowing, expressed emotion.

The world of our emotions is so complex and rich it almost defies description: tides and currents overlapping, intermingling, swelling and subsiding. The shades, nuances and interplay of our emotions seem to be infinite, even in one moment. Our emotional energy is a mighty force if we can harness it. We at Real People Music see the emotions like waves on the ocean. The experience of an emotional 'wave' is your unique self naturally feeling itself. It is a wave of energy that needs to be acknowledged and expressed. We don't need to analyze it. We don't need to change it. Our emotions are just like the ocean's waves that will rise up and then settle down, build up and then subside. As long as we are alive our emotions rise and fall like the ocean's waves.

Emotions are the driving forces of our lives. We do things in order to feel good, and we avoid doing things we think may make us feel pain. We are constantly searching, in every moment, for what will make us feel good, happy and satisfied.

Highly functioning people likely experience happiness and satisfaction on a regular basis. But for many other people, uncontrollable, strong, negative emotions are their constant companions. These 'dark horses' of emotion are always rearing up and getting in the way of any real accomplishment, sabotaging dreams and talents in every way and creating misery in every hour.

Out of desperation and necessity, people may try to contain these 'dark' emotions, stuffing them somewhere, anywhere, so they can get on with the basics of their day-to-day lives. For many, mastering the emotions means constant vigilance, both in trying not to feel and in trying to override emotions with the rational, logical mind. For us at RPM, mastering the emotions means something completely different. We teach people how to 'ride the wave' of emotion with sound and singing instead of trying to mentally wrestle with emotions or trying to stop them after the fact. We want to acknowledge what we're feeling, and, through sound and song, we want to use the inherent energy of that emotion to naturally take us to the place where it will transform itself. And it always will!

What is an emotion? Emotions are how we feel ourselves in our lives. The word itself will tell you how: E-nergy in MOTION. Our emotions are constantly in motion; appearing, disappearing and changing in response to inner and outer stimulus and the interplay between them. In every situation, our emotions are there to tell us what we are feeling in any given moment. Our emotions tell us when things are going well, and when something isn't right. Trouble can come when, unable to find a satisfactory way to progress, unresolved and unexpressed emotions are suppressed or put aside to deal with 'later'. We believe that a backlog of suppressed emotion can make us ill, depressed, and unbalanced, and, if not dealt with, it can kill us.

Once you start suppressing or numbing any emotion - the good, the bad or the ugly, you start numbing them all. You are numbing the ability to feel any emotion, even the 'good' ones. You end up trying to feel something, anything, by hyping yourself and imitating the emotions rather than actually feeling your emotions in your body in real time. By trying to control your emotions, you are taking yourself out of the natural sequence of time.

In this modern world, there are more ways than ever to distract ourselves from what we're really feeling. Alcohol, drugs of all kinds, TV, the Internet, overeating, overspending; the list is endless. We distract our minds and dull our senses; we don't know how to manage our emotional flow.

So, how do we 'deal' with emotions? Emotions can't effectively be dealt with on the level of the mind. We can't think ourselves joyful. An emotion perfectly analyzed by the mind will have no effect on the emotion itself. The emotional energy in itself is not significantly affected by our mental perspective of it. Ultimately, the mind cannot override our emotions, but this is how we are culturally expected to function. It just doesn't work! In creating the perfect plan for our lives, our mind may logically and brilliantly decide the best step for us to take, but despite all our efforts we may not be able to take that step because our darker emotions often get in the way and refuse to do what we tell them to do. This is why so many people are in so much pain. They don't know how to transform the emotions that cause themselves pain. They don't know how to get the energy of those dark emotions to serve them instead of continuing to cripple their lives.

Edwin was once singing a song to an audience of about 300 people at a concert:

Edwin: *"The song was about being very much in love, and that was the feeling that I started with. Halfway through the second verse I suddenly felt depressed, and I began to go through a checklist of everything that was wrong with my life. I began to mentally scroll through my shortcomings and failures to confirm this: I don't exercise enough, my diet is bad, my finances are all over the place, and on and on. I was sinking into a deep hole. All this was happening as I was singing the song. Suddenly I felt afraid I was losing the audience so I kicked up the tempo, creating an upbeat gospel groove to finish the song. Leaving the stage to a round of applause, I sat down next to a woman who said to me, 'Edwin, your song reminded me of when I used to be in love and it made me feel miserable."*

Knowing what he knows now, Edwin would have acknowledged the great sadness in the room while he was singing and been able to use that energy. This would have naturally created empathy with the audience and indeed with himself. He now knows that the direction and intention of that song is to wake up the magical innocence of love. He realized that probably the greater part of the audience was not experiencing this level of love in their lives. They were dealing with things like divorce, heartbreak, death, and loneliness - all kinds of misery. As Edwin sang the song to them, these feelings of pain began to come up in the room. They were coming up because they needed to be healed so that love could flow again. Had he acknowledged that emotion of sadness while he was singing, it would have naturally started to transform. It would have been given voice. Instead he actually made that emotion of sadness 'wrong' and forced it into a more acceptable feeling that he thought everybody would like. The art is to accept the emotions as they come up, and then you'll find that their energy has been freed to take you to wherever you want to go. It will always take you to a better place.

Edwin: *"I had a conversation with a woman once who was close to a spiritual Master. She also had the ability to see subtle levels of peoples' energy patterns. She indicated to the Master that his security guards had very dark, controlling energy. The Master answered, 'Yes, I know, but they're very useful.' This story is brilliant because even though they themselves were not ready to change, the Master was able to use their dark emotional energy as a force to serve good rather than trying to change them. Powerful people are not afraid of the dark side of life. They use it for good."*

Emotions are incredibly strong and refuse to be ignored for very long. Don't we all know it! Ultimately, emotions refuse not to be acknowledged, and will make all kinds of trouble for us until they are acknowledged.

Part of the acknowledgment process means we must develop an emotional vocabulary. Most of us have a rudimentary emotional vocabulary at best, not having learned it when we were young. We would say that the absence of an emotional vocabulary is epidemic, at least in English-speaking countries. At Real People Music, our definition of 'emotional vocabulary' is to be able to attach non-judgmental words to our emotional feelings for the purpose of understanding and sharing what we are feeling. Many people can't recognize their real emotions because they don't have a solid emotional vocabulary. For instance, we always ask people to tell us what they feel in their bodies, but the response is almost always description-based: it's hollow, it's stressed, it's energized, or they start to explain the reason for it. So when we ask them what that emotion is, very often they cannot clearly qualify it. They can't say that they feel excited, happy, sad, frustrated, angry, apprehensive, uncertain or fearful, because they don't have the association with the language to express how they feel. Their mind hasn't associated these emotions with the feelings within their body. They are detached from their true emotions.

In a perfect world our parents would have taught us all about emotional vocabulary, about how to clearly identify what we are feeling. But even with a small emotional vocabulary we can transform the energy of our dark emotions through sound and singing. And this will help us on our way to developing a rich emotional vocabulary and emotional mastery in life.

We've met many people who are afraid of their emotions and people who feel that they are barely clinging on to a semblance of normalcy. They are afraid that if they were to encourage emotional expression, if they were to let go even inadvertently, something terrible would happen.

We have found the opposite to be true: that the natural release of that inner censure in the context of sound and song results in feelings of freedom, joy and profound relief. It results in the transformation of dark, churning emotional energy to peace and self-understanding. And it usually happens fast.

Rather than using the usual socially accepted approach of trying to change emotions, to cover up emotions, to control the emotions, to have the perfect emotion, or project the emotion that we think is suitable, we are doing the opposite; we are accepting any emotion that comes along, recognizing that this is the emotion the body needs to feel in order to heal itself. This does not mean that when anger comes up in a love song, that the love song will sound angry. It might, but not necessarily; that anger is just energy and can colour the sound in many ways. It is the body's energy coming up as an emotion to heal itself.

So again, how do we deal with emotions? When you listen to people talking about their emotions, they say "I feel…, I feel…., I feel…." Here is a great truth: emotions aren't floating around in our mental atmospheres, they are literally felt in our bodies.

When we first present this concept in our seminars, Edwin starts simply by asking people to remember a time in their lives when something made them feel very happy. Then he asks them to put their attention on their bodies and find the particular place where that feeling of happiness is located. It is always the case that there will be a specific bodily location for any emotional state.

Having said that, the location of any feeling in the body can and will change; one day, a certain happiness may be felt in the centre of the chest, another day happiness may be felt in the belly. There are no rules about which feelings 'belong' in which area of the body; any sensation of emotion may be felt anywhere in the body at any time. For some people the sensation is as powerful as a beacon, and for others the sensation might not be so obvious at first, but perhaps only a very slight fluttering feeling. We've found that the more people experiment and practice with feeling and identifying the connection between body and emotions, the clearer and easier it becomes. This is an essential tool for any singer, any speaker, or for anyone wanting emotional mastery.

Every emotion can be described as a wave of a particular type of energy – a wave of happiness, love, fear, anger or whatever. It doesn't matter what kind of wave it is, we've discovered there are certain simple and natural principles that govern our emotional wave's behaviour. It's just like surfing, and we invite you to become a master at riding the waves of your emotions!

Principle: Even without realizing it, we are always seeking a state of emotional balance. The natural state of emotional balance is a state of radiant peace and calm, maintained without effort in the nervous system. Using our ocean wave analogy, we represent this state of emotional balance as the seashore where all the highs and lows of our emotional waves naturally come to rest. It is the nature of the wave to reach the shore, just as it is the nature of every emotion to find balance. Just as the inherent energy of the wave naturally carries it toward the shore, the energy inherent in an emotion will carry itself to a state of balance if we don't disrupt the natural process.

Principle: We can learn to 'surf' our emotional waves through sound, song and movement! It is an extremely powerful, effective, and in-the-moment way of bringing our past and present emotions into balance in the time it takes to sing a song, usually under four minutes! As a surfer on the sea of emotion, we teach you how to stay 'on top' of the emotional wave and keep 'riding' it. By a simple process, and by our emotion's nature and inherent energy, it will be driven to the inner calm shore, that place of emotional balance, and become still. The emotional wave will have expressed and exhausted its own energy in the process of reaching the shore. And you will feel the thrill of having been able to keep your balance on the top of this powerful and uncontrollable force. You will immediately be more confident and eager to paddle out and catch the next wave in. In being able to 'ride' any challenging emotional wave to the end, you'll gain confidence and experience. You'll be on your way to becoming a master of any emotional wave!

The corollary of this principle is, again using the surfing analogy, if you slip or jump off the wave before it arrives at that calm shore, this is the time where you can really be hurt. You'll find yourself at the mercy of the immense force of the waves, shoved down and tumbling around the bottom of the sea. You'll find yourself being bashed and raked against the coral and the rocks and desperate to reach the surface for a breath of air.

It's the same in our emotional world; if we can't ride the waves of our emotions, we end up bruised, bleeding, treading water and still unable to get to the shore. This is what happens to us when we can't go with our emotional flow. We can't move on, we can't move forward inside. We're stuck out 'at sea', getting more and more exhausted all the while. We'll find that the emotion we weren't able to 'ride' to its peaceful conclusion will continue to haunt us throughout our life until such time as we choose to get on that wave again. At that time we'll have another opportunity to create emotional balance within.

It's actually very easy to ride the waves of emotion. We do it all the time with emotions such as happiness, ecstasy, and joy. We want to savour and experience them to the fullest. We don't want them to end, and often try and hold on to them past the time when they naturally would fade away to make room for the next set of experiences.

It's a different story with the 'darker' emotions, the ones that fill us with feelings of fear, sadness, anger, etc. These feelings can be so uncomfortable and painful that we'll do almost anything in order not to feel them. But in suppressing these emotions, we stop the flow of this energy and prevent its natural transformation and completion. We stop the flow, and in the process we prevent ourselves from getting to that calm, peaceful shore which is always the natural destination of every emotion. To use our surfing analogy, we slip off or jump off the wave somewhere in the middle. Often we then try and hide the fact, pretending we've moved onward and upward, when truthfully we're still churning around at the bottom.

As a human being we have to be able to feel all our emotions and not condemn or be afraid of the dark ones. They are our wake up call to pay attention, our wake up call to action, our wake up call to change something that is unacceptable. You can learn to ride those dark waves and express even the most intense emotions with power and grace. Through song you can use anger, you can use sadness, you can use any emotion to create and express the most deeply moving songs.

When we talk about riding the waves of emotion, we're not talking about trying to keep feeling any particular emotion. We're not talking about deliberately acting out any particular emotion. We're not talking about purposely intensifying any particular emotion. We're not talking about imagining you're on a wave and projecting how any emotion will change. We want to avoid these mental manipulations of emotion, which in every instance takes us out of the natural flow.

The natural flow of emotion follows a law of nature more powerful than the mightiest ocean wave, and like a wave it cannot be controlled by us. The only power we have is to do what it takes to go with that invincible flow. We do not want to control the emotions. We want to experience them and powerfully and gracefully express them. And in the process we find that we are transforming ourselves and our lives beyond anything we might have imagined. We are coming alive more and more. We are feeling more and more 'ourselves', and more and more the person we feel we were meant to be.

Some people might find the idea of not controlling the emotions threatening. They wonder, 'What about all the violence out there? Surely it's madness to encourage people to express it!' We believe that it's the built up emotions of pain, anger, and fear inside people that results in acts of violence. Over the years we've seen thousands of examples of how one song written and sung from the heart and soul can release pain held for a lifetime.

Jennifer S. from Florida, USA, had this to say:

"When you talk about what it's like to 'ride the wave' when you're singing a song, what comes to my mind is this song I'd written about my Dad. I remember singing it after learning how to 'ride the wave', and all this emotion came up. As opposed to holding myself back, I just kind of hung on and literally 'rode the wave'. This was years and years' worth of emotion. This was years and years of crap that I had just not dealt with. It all came up when I was singing. But instead of clamping down and trying to fight it, stuffing it down, or stopping and starting over so that it sounded pretty, Edwin and I ended up going through it anyway. And this voice came out that I didn't know I had, and there was a strength in it that blew my mind. I didn't know that I could sing like that. I didn't know that I could tap into that kind of emotion and survive. It was completely different, and after I learned how to do that, thank God, I've been able to tap into that whenever I record anything. I know that if the emotion comes up, it doesn't have to overwhelm me, but I do have to hang in there with it so I can come out the other side. By 'riding the wave' of emotion when I sing, I

found a depth to my voice that I can't tap into if I don't go there and actually let that emotion fly. I feel that's where my true voice comes out. That's when I can really tap into the God-given voice that I have. And when I feel I don't have to stuff it down, there's a depth that comes out in my voice and moves me, and moves everybody that hears it. Now, I can just go there and it's fantastic. Before, when that emotion would come up, I would think, 'Oh, my gosh, I can't cry, I'm on stage, I'm trying to record,' or whatever; I'd get stuck in my head and then I'd lose the feeling of it. But after I learned that 'ride the wave' technique I could feel myself being able to go with the flow, tapping into this emotion, and I'm basically showing myself raw for people and really tapping into the source of it. And once you do that, it's a beautiful thing; you'll actually hear the voice you've been given, not the one that's been conditioned, not the one that's been trained, not the one that's afraid, but your actual honest-to-God voice. It's a totally different experience. It saved me. That 'ride the wave' concept has saved me on every level. From an emotional standpoint, from a songwriting standpoint, and everything else. It got me through my divorce. It got me through the major shifts I've made in my life this last year. It's got me through all of it."

Principle: It's easy to spontaneously ride the waves of happiness and joy, but there's a technique, a process, needed to help us ride the waves of the 'darker' emotions. Most of us seem to jump or slip off these waves somewhere in the middle. They are just bigger and scarier waves, no doubt taking more skill and courage to ride than we have at that particular moment.

To help anyone ride any emotional wave, we utilize various personal combinations of body awareness, movement, intention, attention, sound, and even visual elements all at the same time as singing a song. What is created is a complex coordination and left/right brain integration event. So many different things are happening at the same time on different levels of the brain, body, voice, senses and psyche. As people go through this exercise, they find that they cannot hold on to any one emotional state. They find themselves going with the flow, riding the wave of emotion, spontaneously able to constantly rebalance themselves as the emotional wave moves beneath them. They are able to keep their internal balance while remaining in the natural flow of the emotion.

Using body awareness, people are reminded that emotions are a constantly changing physical reality. Body awareness also utilizes the mind to deeply focus on the emotion as it transforms. Maintaining body awareness helps us to stay with the changing emotion, and keeps the mind occupied and focused. Body awareness helps us to feel inside our body.

Moving our body keeps things moving forward, frees physical energy, builds coordination and prevents us from becoming stuck and disconnected from the flow of the emotional wave. Moving our body keeps us on the wave. Movement helps us to feel our bodies moving in space.

Making sound expresses the layers of emotion within the wave, creating vibration inside and outside the body. With this sound we have the intention to ride the wave of emotion and follow it as it transforms on its own. We become aware of the finer levels of emotion and wake up to the powerful natural impetus of emotional energy. By making sound, we can ride and experience the transformation of any wave of emotion.

Being able to ride the waves of emotion has profound consequences for the body as well, because, as we said before, we hold emotion in our bodies. When you can bring your emotions into balance, your body spontaneously becomes more balanced, too. And when the body is released from the hold of negative emotions, it is more relaxed, less stressed, and it has more energy available to heal itself.

How about: Singing a few lines of a simple song you know well, just a minute or so. Where do you feel this song in your body? Where is your attention drawn? Where is the emotional response or sensation in your body? Although the head is a part of your body, for now, do not include any sensations in the head. These feelings will be mirrored in the body anyway. Once you've found an area of feeling in the body, place your hands on it and ask the question, while keeping your attention on the body location: how does my body want to move/dance here if it was free to do so right now? Go ahead, move/dance, and as you're doing this, sing the song again. This is not a performance for any imagined audience, this is an experience just for you. An experience of feeling an emotion, and learning to 'get on the wave' through movement, sound and song.

"This Field of Unbounded Emotional Energy is the new frontier for singing, for all the arts, and for living life in the fullest capacity. It was unknown and now it is known. Engaging with it guarantees your life is transformed."

Cheryl Coppard

Chapter 5

The Field of Unbounded Emotional Energy and the Unbounded Voice

Chapter 5

The Field of Unbounded Emotional Energy and the Unbounded Voice

Cheryl: *"I recently made a mind boggling discovery which has opened our eyes once again to the magic and mystery of nature, the human being, and the power of singing. I was doing my morning singing workout; that is, moving and making sound, when I realized I wasn't feeling any emotion. And at that moment I realized this was unnatural.*

I realized that I had unconsciously blocked the flow of emotion. I then had an innocent thought to let the emotional energy flow freely. Suddenly my voice became alive in a way I'd never experienced before. The sound that came out was incredibly powerful and full of resonance, nuance and passion, probably at least twenty times what it was before. My body buzzed with energy and I was overwhelmed with feelings of joy. I immediately realized that this was the 'zone' of singing. It was effortless once I was in it and over the next 3 months Edwin and I have proven to ourselves that it is 100% consistent; every day when we sing, we sing in the zone. We have begun teaching this, and everyone we've taught since has had an experience of this, though not always as dramatic or not always as instant."

The experience is so powerful, so distinct, and yet so abstract that it has taken us several months using ourselves as guinea pigs to discover what this field of unbounded emotional energy is all about, and also to find the proper language to describe it. Although we are completely confident with our results, we doubt we will ever understand the mechanics.

What was clear from the beginning was that this field of unbounded emotional energy was not personal but universal. It was clear that this field of unbounded emotional energy is comprised of latent emotion only; that is, within itself it exhibits no quality of emotion. It is like light that only gets separated into specific colours when shining through a prism. In the case of a human being experiencing emotion, the prism is our body, our psyche, and our soul. As the clear, unbounded emotional energy flows through us, it becomes coloured by our experiences past and present. Those colours then shine through our lives as the kaleidoscope of emotions we experience on a day-to-day basis. These colours shine through our voices as well.

It was also clear from Cheryl's experience that this field of unbounded emotional energy was intimately connected with nature. She recognized that this unbounded emotional energy comes from nature itself, and was actually what made nature bursting with the feeling of life. That non-definable, powerful, calming energy that we all take for granted as being the energy of nature. This bursting, abundant, fecund, ‘fully alive’ capacity of nature becomes this latent emotional energy flowing through us all, enabling us to also feel fully alive and express the waves of emotion. To see, to feel how we are part of nature is truly humbling.

That we are connected with nature is logical and obvious. The life on this entire planet is interconnected in profound symbiosis, more knowledge of which is discovered each year. It is an obvious fact that when you go for a walk in the park it makes you feel better, makes you feel good. I now surmise that when people are surrounded by nature they naturally open themselves to this field of unbounded emotional energy. It energizes and cleanses, clearing the mind and opening the heart.

Imagine this energy flowing unimpeded through the voice! Everyone we have taught how to access their Unbounded Voice experiences that the power and the emotional impact of the voice becomes magnified many times. There is no effort, no strain. Peoples’ bodies often subtly, physically, vibrate from all the energy that is passing through their voices.

It was also clear that the voice that sings as a result of connection with this unbounded emotional energy is able to reverberate in an ever-changing infinitude of tones. Every day we sing in this way, the tones in our voices are different from yesterday. Even singing the same song. This is what we experienced for over 3 months when we were initially exploring this phenomenon. Ask any musician - this is extraordinary!

The experience of singing becomes blissful, as stated very powerfully by a woman who attended one of our introductory evening events:

"Edwin gave us a little intro into the Unbounded Voice, how to sing with the whole body, with the unbounded emotional field. We were standing, and feet slightly apart, body relaxed. Nowhere particular in my body did any sensations or blocks come up, but when I opened my mouth to start singing the song, the bottoms of my feet felt like they were golden footprints, and all this soft, delicious energy poured up into my body like my feet were two doors, and it filled up my whole body very quickly and started the bottom chakra resonating, and then the next one, and then the next one all the way up, like my body was hollow, right up through the top of my head, out the top of my head, and it made a big fountain, a golden fountain that draped down over me like a willow tree. Just like that! My body was the trunk and my body was a fountain of light that just flowed all down around me and just kept going down into the ground and coming up again all through my feet like a circulating motion of energy. And of course, I was filled with bliss and joy and love and feeling of 'at home'.

And I noticed that my voice, which is normally quite constrained when I try to sing loudly in a group, was very 'liquid, loveable and wise'. Just easy, energetic, strong, powerful; I felt in tune with my Higher Self.

I had been told three times within the last couple of months by people whose wisdom I value that my 3 bottom energy centres were blocked, that there was stagnant energy there. But when I started the singing, the Unbounded Emotional energy just came roaring up through the top of my head and those energy centres just opened. I could feel them resonating, not shaking or trembling, like that. Just resonating on a quiet level. It was very obvious that they had opened. So that was very nice!

Then Edwin had us stop and he talked a little bit and then we repeated the procedure, and this time, the energy didn't have to come up, it was already up, and my body just disappeared and became transparent, like the walls of a house starting to fade away, fade away, and it was just 'I AM' standing there singing. And that was a revelation, because my Little Self was saying, 'Oh, look at that! You're functioning from wholeness!' I've heard about it, and I've read about it, but it was just so easy! So that was the beginning – first lesson! I'm looking forward to more! " - Christine Clarke-Johnson, USA

And believe it or not, her experience is not unique. We've recently done an event in Japan where a significant number of people described a similar experience.

This discovery is very new, as of June, 2012. We know that in the months and years to come, our experience and understanding of the field of unbounded emotional energy will grow. There will definitely be more to write about the Unbounded Voice!

Because of this breakthrough, we can teach anyone a simple way to tap into the universal field of unbounded emotional energy. Being in the flow of this energy when we sing ensures that our emotions will be expressed in all their beauty and power .We are not managing the specific emotions in any way. The emotions that need to be expressed naturally come up and colour the song. The field of unbounded emotional energy becomes the medium for the complete and total expression of emotion.

And the thing is, the profound complexity of our emotional selves is perfectly, elegantly expressed. For example, if we're singing a sad song, not only will there be the natural emotion of sadness in our tone, there will also naturally be a shifting myriad of tones coming from the layers of other emotions that are connected to our lives at that moment. All this creates incredible, indescribable feelings of richness, both within those who are singing and those who are listening. Goosebumps!

The implications of this new discovery are immense and the questions that come up are, at the moment, equally unassailable. It is obvious to us that it is desirable and essential for the fulfilment of our singing potential to experience and express this field of unbounded emotional energy. We think that this field of unbounded emotional energy can best be accessed through singing. It has also become obvious that through repeated exposure to this field while singing, this field of unbounded emotional energy will naturally, gradually, anchor itself to the rest of our lives and take up permanent residence.

Imagine what it's like to have this energy freely flowing through you at all times! Indeed it has already started for both of us. We have felt many, many changes since we began this journey of the Unbounded Voice, experiencing much personal healing and seeing many changes in both of us.

Cheryl: *"For me, other than the dramatic change in my voice, the most primal shift has been that I feel much more engaged with life, like I'm now in the front row seats, whereas in retrospect, I'd felt like I was up in the bleachers. I had never been aware of my own relationship to life itself, and I'd never felt bothered by its consequences. I'm now seeing my life opening up in such joyous, magical, and unexpected way. I foresee this new discovery opening up the emotional experience of humanity on a large scale in the near future. It's almost beyond the reach of imagination what will unfold from the global reawakening of the field of unbounded emotional energy in everyone's lives!!"*

"A bird doesn't sing because it has an answer, it sings because it has a song."

Maya Angelou, American Poet, b.1928

Chapter 6

Songs and Song Writing

Chapter 6

Songs and Song Writing

All around the Earth it is still the most natural thing in the world to sing soothing songs to babies and young children - lullabies. This is usually the beginning of our experience of the power of song. The love in a mother's voice, what is more powerful than that?

Then as adults, many people cherish a dream of being able to stand up and confidently sing their favourite songs in front of others. That's why they often come to us. But people always get more than they bargained for because, within a few hours, we have them writing and singing their own songs!

Edwin: *"In the middle of the night, sometime in 1990, Cheryl woke me up and excitedly told me that she was sure we could teach people how to write their own songs. The light bulb went on! I instinctively knew she was right on track, and the next day we were experimenting with the process."*

Songs come from within us, and our instinct was that they came from the same place as the voice. If that pure voice comes from that connection with the body, pure songs are also going to come from that same place. They are going to come from the body. The most powerful, most creative songs don't come from a preconceived idea of what you want to say, or from poetry made up to rhyme. Experience has shown us that beautiful songs are already alive inside us, words and melody, and will come out almost effortlessly once we access that deep place inside. The key is to be able to get out of the way.

We use a simple process to tap people into that experience of writing songs from the body. It's remarkable what starts to happen. These songs just start pouring out of people, and characteristically they say things like, 'Wow, I've never written words like this before; I've never even said anything like this before.' We've had clients who can't stop writing songs once they've learned how, some even write hundreds of songs! It seems that every time they have a few minutes to spare, another song bubbles up. Once they've opened the door, it seems there is so much that still needs to be expressed. We've had professional singer/songwriters tell us that this way of song writing, and the songs that come out of it, are strikingly different from their usual style.

Edwin: *"I heard a story about a ritual practiced by a tribe somewhere, I forget where. Someone in this tribe was behaving in an inappropriate manner. He or she would be asked to come and sit in the middle of a circle of the tribespeople. The person was then asked this one question, 'What is left unsaid?' This story struck me as being so poignant. My assumption is that in those circumstances, the person was allowed to say anything without judgment, punishment, recrimination, or criticism. They were just listened to. What is left unsaid? What do you need to say still?*

This tribe had created a ritual in an environment that allowed that person to keep speaking until he or she felt free. Until he or she had really gotten down to the bottom of what really needed to be said; in other words, had in that process been able to come to a truth that they had somehow suppressed inside themselves. The truth really does set you free, physically, mentally, emotionally and spiritually. When I reflected on this story I immediately got this beautiful picture that this is what we are doing when we teach people to write and sing their own songs. People always end up expressing what has too long been left unsaid. From our perspective, songs do the same thing as words but even more powerfully. They express the unsaid. They bring us to the truth about ourselves."

Our point of entry into song writing is the body. We've said how the body holds emotion, but another way of saying this is that the body holds layers of memory. Think about it: think about a singular traumatic incident as a child; say, watching your parents have a terrible argument. In addition to witnessing the argument with your eyes and hearing it with your ears, you're definitely feeling something in the body at the same time - maybe it makes you feel sick to your stomach. You may still feel it even after so many years. Or, think about a singular incident that held great magic and joy. Again, in addition to the experiences from the other senses, you're definitely feeling something in the body at the same time. Our feeling body remembers everything we've experienced even if our minds have stored it away, long forgotten. It is this body memory that becomes the key, the sacred treasure trove of material for our songs and our own unfolding.

Years and decades of teaching this way of song writing has proven to us that all the songs people write end up bringing them some realization, some perspective about themselves. It is not only the intellectual or emotional realizations that we may get, but by singing the sounds of our song, we give the body/mind a vehicle to actually really heal itself. Singing your own song creates a sequence of sound vibrating throughout your body. We believe this self-generated vibration has the effect of transforming the physical level where memories, or the impacts of experience, are being held. We believe that this sequence of sound that we first sing to ourselves is naturally one of the body's ways of bringing itself to balance. The song we're finally singing about the death of a loved one will sequentially vibrate through our bodies. It will unerringly find that knot of grief in the chest and shake it loose. That grief begins to dissolve and we shine brighter for it. The sounds of our songs shake loose the beauty of our soul!

During our events, we create an environment where people feel free to express what they need to; to express whatever may come up. But rather than through speaking, we guide people to bring out their poetry through their songs. Once the process is begun, all they need to do is stay with the flow inside.

We do not judge anything that comes from this creative process. We are not trying to get people to remember anything or recreate any particular experience. We are not trying to get people to write a hit song. People are not logically trying to write a song with a verse, chorus, bridge, or with any other kind of format. They are just simply writing from a place inside that they feel connected to at that time, without any agenda in terms of structure or content. People don't have to worry about trying to create a song. The thing we've found is that everyone carries the structure of a song within themselves. We've never met anyone who couldn't write and sing their own song.

Cheryl: *"What comes out are these very pure and beautiful songs which can literally set a person free. The first time we tried this process within a group, I started writing some words that seemed nonsensical to me at first. Curious, I stuck to the process and kept writing, and, when I about halfway into the piece of poetry, I realized what it was about. It ended up being a very powerful emotional experience for me, and completely unexpected. The experience I had is typical of what most people go through at some point in this process."*

During our song writing process, the body memory is given the chance to write the words, rather than the mind. We focus on what is actually being felt in the body in the moment rather than what the mind might be thinking or wishing. What comes out on the paper is some potent inner truth, often even hidden from our conscious mind, expressing what had been too long left unsaid.

The story, the poetry of the words, is the core of the song. Without the story, there is only a melody. The melody might be exquisite, but alone it has little connection to our personal history. It is the poetry and the music together that makes a song so powerful. For most people, the words of the song come first. They come from inside with a particular flavour and rhythm. From the interaction between flavour and rhythm the melody arises. But it can also be the other way; for some people, the words of the song seem to come out of the melody. They listen very deeply to the melody they've found inside, and hear the poetry embedded within it. Either way a song is born!

When we've written this amazing song we need to share it. If there were no one to listen, a lot of the joy would go out of it. In fact, we wonder if we can really know anyone until we've heard them sing their own song. We believe that when you sing your own song you express the most complete and full expression of what is inside you at that time. The sound and resonance of each voice is so unique. We don't really hear it when people talk. It is the singing voice that brings out the deeper levels of expression. And it is the story of the song that creates connection and appreciation for who we are and for what we've been through.

Songs can also bring us what we need. In the movie 'Australia' the aboriginal boy says he will sing Nicole Kidman's character to him. We believe there is truth in this. For example, think of what the song 'Let it Be' might have brought to Sir Paul McCartney, and indeed is still bringing to him. Can you imagine what the influence of that one song attracted and brought to him over his life so far? It is really beautiful, really profound, what the energy of a song can create for us.

Edwin*: " One of our clients, PF, attended our 6-day advanced training in Tofino, Canada. She wrote a song that started with the words, ' Ooh, I'm hungry for a man...' Every time she sang it, it was almost perfect, but there was always something not quite complete. After the course, she continued to take personal sessions with me. We tried all kinds of wild things, having her sing it to her mother, to her father, to her sister, and much more. Every time, the song had some magic, but still didn't feel complete. Then one day Cheryl suggested that PF sit in a chair in the middle of the room and describe how she saw herself. She said, 'I am very plain.' As she explored this, she started to cry as she felt the pain of that statement. Before our eyes, her deep inner feminine beauty came to the surface. I looked up and hardly recognized her. A different woman had appeared in the room and she looked radiant. She sang the song again and it was perfect! The following week when she came for another session, she had a glint in her eyes. I said, 'What's up?' She said, 'He's arrived!' She had manifested a partner with her song."*

When songs become completely integrated, they manifest. We've seen it happen often with so many clients.

Your songs are your legacy. They tell the unique stories of your life in your inimitable style with your inimitable sound. Your songs become your tools for personal expression, transformation, and manifestation. By bringing out any feeling that may be inside and transforming it into a song, you may be surprised to find that you've created something of surprising profundity. Think about it. Many people have a lot of pain inside them. What a gift to yourself to transform that pain so gracefully into a song. Creating such a song is a testament to our ability as human beings to transform something deeply painful into something whole, something of profound beauty. And in the singing of it you will reinforce that wholeness within yourself and also within anyone who hears it.

The following song, the Queen of Darkness, was written by Niedra Gabriel from the USA, who went, in 5 days, from someone who had never written a song in her life to a woman who now wants to write, choreograph, and perform in a musical production with this song somewhere in it. She had this to say:

"I decided on a whim to join Edwin and Cheryl's 5-day course, 'Your Voice is the Messenger of Your Soul'. I was tired of working on myself, and something in me said, "This is probably the most creative education you could do and if you want to be an artist – GO!

I had always been creative; I'd trained and worked as a ballet dancer, done choreography, taught yoga, dance and movement. I became one of the top Pilates instructors in LA. Yet there was a part of me always frustrated. I had never fully experienced what I had inside - it had all been done in silence. I never felt that I touched on or expressed my core as an artist. The decision was made – a week later I was on a plane to Canada, going to find out what is going on with me - who am I really?

The training was about getting into my body (done that), with sound (never done that), with inner truth (done that), without technique or rules or structure (oh, my God), and with lots and lots of self-expression written into songs (I don't recognize myself – I'm losing my mind!).

The day we were to write our Sovereign song – the song that was to express who we are and why we are here (in this world) - I was feeling quite freaked out. All the structure was gone and I was left with myself. I was in pain and surrounded by the blackest cloud of depression I had ever experienced, reminiscent of my teenage days when I was still directly in touch with my dream of becoming a great dancer and yet frozen by fears and insecurities of ever fulfilling that dream or myself.

In my adult life I have struggled and worked on that aspect of my personality forever – looking to change / get rid of / evolve out of / deny / that part of me that is sure that I will fail and destroy anything that I desire. Here I was supposed to be surging forward with creativity, and every dredge of my 'stuff' was alive and screaming in my face.

Voicing my state to Cheryl, she very gently suggested I follow the song writing process and write a song about what was going on inside. I walked away feeling alone and in despair, wanting to destroy everything - I would never get through this!

As I sat by myself, I glanced up and looked at my emotional darkness, and with amazement watched a Queen manifest out of the dark! I knew her so well, I actually loved her, she was powerful, she was part of me, she had a voice and I had always kept her from speaking. This time she spoke and I wrote The Queen of Darkness.

That was a turning point for me. In an instant I became free, I was complete and I had found my shadow. I had reached into my demons and found they were my friends - they had been monsters because I never let them have a voice.

The rest was a dream-come-true. I sang my song to the group and got a standing ovation. I went on to record my song with Real People Music – a most fulfilling experience for an artist who never had anything left of her art once it was manifested.

Most of all I found I could contact and use my creative vision - any time, any place, in any modality, so fast and so fluidly because I no longer had to be in any preconceived state to create. I found that who I am right now is the most perfect vehicle for expressing my soul-- however dark she wants to be today."

The Queen of Darkness – Niedra Gabriel

I am the Queen, the Queen of darkness
Personify your darkest fears
Every hope and wish you cherish
I pull apart I crush to tears

When you reach for light to guide you
I pull the switch I close you down
And when you think you walk your journey
I twist and turn your road around

And now you think you are so special
You are not I'll show you why
Each time you reach you reach for freedom
I squeeze your soul don't let you fly

Ha Ha Ha I laugh insanely
As I see you find your way
Not so you foolish little Earthling
I just turned the sign that way

So sleep my dear and pray to angels
There is no hope there's nothing here
It's all a hoax a way to trap you
To hold you down to keep you here

I am the Queen the Queen of darkness
I sit my throne I hold your reins
So walk alone don't look behind you
Your shadow self points to the way

How about: Considering songs that have influenced your life? Remember them and what was happening in your life at that time. How did they influence and encapsulate your life experience?

"The more one sees of human fate and the more one examines its secret springs of action, the more one is impressed by the strength of unconscious motives and by the limitations of free choice"

Carl Gustav Jung Swiss psychiatrist,
Psychologist 1875-1961

Chapter 7

The Living Archetypal World Inside Us

Chapter 7

The Living Archetypal World Inside Us

We made our way to the world of the Living Archetypes via the unlikely route of sound, singing and song. We have not studied the literature of archetype and mythology at University. One weekend seminar based on a book started us off on this part of our journey in the 1990s. The book is called King, Warrior, Magician, Lover - Rediscovering the Archetypes of the Mature Masculine, by Robert Moore and Douglas Gillette, and was published by HarperCollins in 1990. We are full of gratitude towards these two men for their brilliant work.

Edwin found something deeply compelling about the Archetypal model that was presented during that weekend. He was fascinated and wanted to explore it further in his own way. He began to experiment with the concept in the context of our own work, that of sound and song. What he found was sensational: that like the voice and the songs, the primordial Archetypal energies exist inside our own bodies as much as they exist in our psyches or our minds.

We discovered that these archetypes are immediate, personified, fully alive, and evolving within us throughout our lives. That is why we are calling them the Living Archetypes. They really are alive inside us! We have also found through experience that anyone and everyone can easily access, express, empower, and bring to balance their own Living Archetypes using the vehicles of sound and song.

We believe that the four primordial Living Archetypes - Sovereign, Lover, Magician, and Warrior - are the four essential parts of each of us. The four parts of our psyche. We found that they were designed to be connected together, like puzzle pieces. If the pieces of a puzzle are fitted together the image makes sense. If we can't fit the pieces together, even though each piece may be interesting and beautiful, we will never see the picture that was intended. It's the same with our psyche and our lives. If the four parts of our psyche are not able to synergy together as one, the Big Picture of our lives cannot be seen or lived by us. If our Living Archetypes are functioning together, it means that our soul, our hearts, our minds, and our ability to act are all naturally and easily working together. The Big Picture of our lives can be created and lived!

Cheryl: *"I had a session with a woman, JW from Canada, who had great heaviness and pain in her heart regarding her two grown sons. Since she'd divorced their father, they didn't call or come around. She'd tried many times over the last five years to initiate connection but to no avail. Together, over a few hours, JW and I went through the internal world of her Living Archetypes. By the end of the session, JW felt a peaceful awareness within herself which, she later told me, blossomed into three days of an altered reality of expanded, blissful, universal wholeness. For her, this was fulfilment in itself, but within two days of the session both her sons independently called her, wanting to come over, wanting to invite her to dinner. She had done nothing except shift her internal landscape."*

In 1960 Napoleon Hill published his landmark book 'Think and Grow Rich', a how-to book on maximizing personal achievement. We believe that he also discovered this Archetypal world inside himself. In his book, he details how, for many years, in the interest of rebuilding his character, he held nightly meetings with his "Invisible Counsellors". He decided to use the nine men he admired most as his invisible counsellors: Emerson, Paine, Edison, Darwin, Lincoln, Burbank, Napoleon, Ford and Carnegie. He deeply admired the essence of their gifts, but equally what they did with those gifts.

From our point of view, each of these exceptional men was representing one of Napoleon Hill's own internal Living Archetypes, with the essence of one particular Archetype strongly coming through in everything each man stood for. All the Archetypes are represented, though it seems he gave more weight to the Lover and Sovereign.

Napoleon Bonaparte, a French military and political leader who came into power near the end of the French Revolution, represents the Warrior. Napoleon Bonaparte is generally acknowledged as one of the greatest military geniuses in all history. Napoleon Hill wanted to emulate Bonaparte's ability to turn defeat into victory, to overcome great obstacles, and to inspire men to greater action. The Warrior is all about action.

Thomas Edison, well-known inventor, represents the Magician. One of the most prolific inventors in history, Edison took out 1,093 US patents in his name. Napoleon Hill wanted to emulate Edison's faith and the persistence it took to uncover nature's secrets. Henry Ford, American automaker, also represents the Magician. He and his company invented automated production -one of his cars could be assembled in one hour and 33 minutes, as opposed to the few cars per day of the previous method. His company was also the first in franchising, profit sharing, and other innovations. Napoleon Hill wanted to emulate Ford's persistence, determination and organizing power. The Magician is all about processing information, invention, and what if…?

Ralph Waldo Emerson, an American poet and essayist represents, for us, the Lover. He is well known for writing about the spiritual potential of human beings, how we can realize; that is, make real, almost anything. His belief that the Universe is composed of Nature and the Soul fully resonates with the feeling of unbounded connection that is the Lover's gift to each of us. Napoleon Hill admired Emerson and wished to emulate his understanding of nature and his understanding and ability to adapt himself to the laws of nature.

Charles Darwin, English naturalist, author of 'The Origin of Species' also represents the Lover. His discovery of how life evolves through natural selection unifies the life sciences and explains life's diversity. He explored very deeply the connections between species. Napoleon Hill wanted to emulate Darwin's patience and unbiased ability to study cause and effect. Luther Burbank, an American botanist, horticulturalist and a pioneer in agricultural science, also represents the Lover. Before the time of genetically modified organisms, he developed and hybridized more than 800 varieties of plants over his career, mostly food plants, creating more and better crops. Napoleon Hill wanted to emulate Burbank's ability to harmonize the laws of nature. The Lover is all about love of nature and connection with all things.

Abraham Lincoln, 16th president of the USA, represents the Sovereign. He led the country through the Civil War, preserving its union, ending slavery, and promoting modernization. Napoleon Hill desired to emulate Lincoln's sense of justice and human understanding. Thomas Paine, one of the founding fathers of the USA, also represents the Sovereign. He advocated a World peace organization, anti-slavery, and social security for the poor and elderly. Hill wished to emulate Paine's freedom of thought, and his courage and clarity in expressing his convictions.

Andrew Carnegie, a Scottish-American industrialist and entrepreneur who was also a philanthropist, also represents the Sovereign. With his great wealth he founded endowments for peace, education, the Arts, and museums not only in the USA, but in Canada, the UK and other countries. Even here in Victoria, BC, Canada, one of the oldest buildings in town is a beautiful stone structure named The Carnegie Library! Napoleon Hill desired to emulate Carnegie's principles of organized effort. The Sovereign is all about the big picture, with the wholeness being more than the sum of the parts.

Let us synthesize, in terms of the Living Archetypes, what Napoleon Hill wanted to emulate in each of these great men. His Warrior: ability to turn defeat into victory, to overcome great obstacles, and to inspire men to greater action. His Magician: faith and the persistence it took to uncover nature's secrets. Also determination and organizing power. His Lover: understanding of nature and the understanding and ability to adapt himself to the laws of nature. Also patience, and an unbiased ability to study cause and effect. Also, the ability to harmonize the laws of nature. His Sovereign: justice and human understanding, freedom of thought, and courage and clarity in expressing his convictions. Also, the principles of organized effort.

It is very clear to us that he created a model for himself whereby he could nightly edify his Warrior, Magician, Lover and Sovereign to 'reshape' his character, to become all he could be. These were the qualities he was telling his Living Archetypes that he wanted strengthened in himself. From what we've come to know about the inner realm of the Living Archetypes, there is an exact correlation between what he asked of each of his Living Archetypes and their intrinsic ability to provide it.

Napoleon Hill, after the first several months of holding these meetings with his "Invisible Counsellors" was astounded that they had become 'real'. He gives the example that Lincoln developed a habit of being late, and that Burbank and Paine often enjoyed witty exchanges. In fact, Napoleon Hill discontinued these meetings for several months because they were so realistic and uncanny, and he became afraid of their consequences. Nevertheless, he got over his fear and did go on to make these meetings a lifelong habit, even if he still regarded his counsellors as imaginary. The way he describes it, during these meetings he became more receptive to knowledge that reached him through the 'sixth sense', what he explained as "Infinite Intelligence voluntarily communicating with the individual."

Napoleon Hill relates that on numerous occasions, some life threatening, he was miraculously guided past difficulty by his "Invisible Counsellors". He goes on to say that using his counsellors became a strategy with every difficult problem both for himself and for his clients.

Although he continued to categorize his "Invisible Counsellors" as imaginary, he says they led him "into glorious paths of adventure" (We'd call this awakening the Warrior), "emboldened the expression of honest thought" (We'd call this awakening the Magician),"encouraged creative endeavours" (We'd call this awakening the Lover), and "rekindled an appreciation of true greatness" (We'd call this awakening the Sovereign).

Napoleon Hill considered the principle of the sixth sense and the "Invisible Counsellors" that made it real the apex of his teaching. He considered that one could only understand it and master it after having mastered the other twelve principles that came before it, explained in the twelve previous chapters of his book, 'Think and Grow Rich', published by Fawcett-Crest in 1960 and Ballantine Books in 1983.

We have found a way to make it easy to find and interact with your Living Archetypes. It is not necessary to master any body of knowledge before embarking upon this journey.

All our experience with ourselves and thousands of clients tells us emphatically that the world he discovered inside is not imaginary, it is the world of the Living Archetypes and is just as real as the world of the conscious mind that most people live in. It is so beautiful to read about his innocent discovery and his reaction to it. It is also so affirming to us to see the results that he got over the course of his life connecting to this internal world of the Living Archetypes.

Napoleon Hill unknowingly began his inner Living Archetypal journey with the idea of strengthening and reshaping his character by creating his ultimate internal advisory board. It ended up working beyond his wildest dreams! And the reason, from our point of view, was that he was nightly creating connection, communication, and synergy between the highest potentials, as he saw them, of his own Living Archetypes. He was so one-pointed, sincere and unshakeable in his beliefs and his actions that it resulted in his worldly success as well. By the year he died, 1970, Napoleon Hill's book, 'Think and Grow Rich' had sold 20 million copies and is still one of the best selling books of all time.

Most of us want to live up to our highest potential and spend a lot of our time, energy and money to strengthen and reshape our characters. It is extremely difficult changing habits and beliefs on the level of the conscious mind! Changing them on the level of the Living Archetypes is much, much easier! Voyaging within the realm of the Living Archetypes creates balance inside. Negative transforms into positive. Something is created that you can build upon. It's like good health: when you are suffering, you are constantly aware of your suffering. Then when you become well, you forget what it was like to suffer. You take for granted the state of good health. We don't think about it anymore, we just live the life of a healthy person. A negative pattern is changed and we don't have to concern ourselves with it any more. We just move forward with our lives.

Sei-chan from Japan writes about how a few hours of focus in the realm of the Living Archetypes changed the habit of a lifetime: *"I had been to my parents' place this summer, a few weeks after the session and found myself a lot different than before.*

My father has a habit of putting himself in the position of the victim; in other words, he tries to make it look like other people are always the abusers. Whenever he acted like that, I used to get angry with him or feel guilty for being mad. But this time, though he hadn't changed, I didn't feel triggered at all! This is such a big step forward for me!

During the Living Archetype session with Cheryl, I had an 'aha!' experience in the realm of the Lover Archetype and realized I am not responsible for other peoples' lives. We are all living our own life. I do not have to put others' needs before mine all the time. I only help them when it's needed. I have more important things to focus on! The time in my life is not infinite and I want to do, to learn, and to grow much more for myself! I realized I'm not being selfish, I'm only being true to myself. Putting one's energy into one's own life is what we are meant to do in this life time."

Cheryl*: "Here is another example of shifting a very deep pattern in a few hours from the realm of the Living Archetypes. I had a session with Minori, a woman from Japan, on the subject of the illness and death of her father 25 years ago. It was continuing to affect her to a disproportionate degree. Through interaction with her Living Archetypes, she was able to see, to have the visceral experience, that she had never processed the emotions. She had tried to be strong for the rest of her family. She had pretended she was OK. She was able to see how, in the big picture, her father showed the family how to live with his way of dying. He gave them a chance to think about life and death. She was able to profoundly feel that her father still loved her and her family very much, and is always beside them with love. She was able to listen to her Sovereign's advice: 'Trust your intuition and go with the flow without doubt. You are on the right path.' She feels as though she has shed this weighty baggage surrounding her father's death, feeling free and light. She also saw that she wants to help people with low self-confidence. Twenty-five years of being so overshadowed by her father's death - released in a few hours!"*

It's in having the visceral experience, the mind/body experience, the 'aha' experience, that allows the pathways of memory to be freed, the suppressed energy to be released, and at the same time allows a holistic understanding to dawn. We believe this is the mechanics of real personal growth and the internalisation of real knowledge. The realm of the Living Archetypes is where this visceral experience occurs. It's a place where real self-understanding dawns. It's a place where negative habits and beliefs are transformed into life supporting ones.

When people are introduced to this world of the Living Archetypes, for most it is a revelation, because they finally begin to understand experientially why they have conflicting inner needs, desires, and points of view. They start to see and understand why they have always had some kind of war going on inside. They start to see their lifelong struggles and challenges in perspective. They start to experience that peace and order can be created out of their inner chaos in a quick and elegant way. They start to see and understand others in a new light. With our RPM program they experience how these inner realities easily begin to be shifted. The beauty of our RPM program is that we use simple tools and techniques to bring the team of the Living Archetypes together in an unexpected, visceral, natural, graceful, profound, and outrageously fun way.

To our way of thinking, there will never be practical benefits in leaving these archetypes in any book. They are so much more than just an idea; they are the living architecture of our psyches! They are the facets of our soul. Because no matter how smart we are, no matter how diligently we may strive to perfectly mould our thoughts and behaviours to the ideals promoted in any book or from any source outside ourselves, ultimately we cannot succeed. Those beautiful and elegant ideas are destined and doomed to remain in our intellects, in our minds, like every other memorable book we may have read. Why? Because they have no immediate, personal, functioning connection in the body, no connection to our own visceral experience. To our way of thinking, the tools we need to expand, express, and transform ourselves cannot be realized from the information in any book. We need to have a mind/body experience as well. This is the only way knowledge is truly realized. Memorizing information, training our minds, is one thing, but spontaneously living it is quite another.

After learning about the Archetypes, Edwin immediately started to experiment with the physical energies of the Living Archetypes by identifying, finding, and waking up these specific energies in the body. He started doing this by instinct and intuition and was immediately amazed by our clients' responses. He had already been having tremendous success bringing out peoples' voices and songs by processes of bringing them back to the body. And now we are also bringing the primordial energies of the Sovereign, Lover, Magician and Warrior out of books and into our awareness of our own bodies and integrating that experience with the voice. These Living Archetypes are not external, but internal!

Edwin: *"When I first started working with the Archetypes with my clients I used very basic techniques. I would just say, for instance, 'On a scale of 1-10, what is the energy level of your Warrior?' The client would say, '4 or 5' and I would say, 'Wake it up!' He would say, 'How?' and I would say, 'Dance, move, sing, increase the energy.' After 5 or 10 minutes the client was at a '10' and his presence had dramatically changed. His voice was completely different. One client spontaneously created a ritual, walking back and forth across the room, brandishing an imaginary sword, and chanting the words, 'Slash and burn!' The thing was, when he came in the following week, he reported that he'd never gotten so much done in a week. He'd even cleaned up his extremely messy office! This made sense because the Warrior is all about taking action, even destroying what is not needed so that a new level of order can arise. He'd definitely woken his Warrior up."*

In the process of becoming aware of the condition of our internal Living Archetypes we are realizing the nature and structure of our own psyches. Through the programs we offer at RPM, people are experiencing the physical connection to their sound, the physical connection to their voice, the physical connection to their own songs, and the physical connection to their Living Archetypes. The results are nothing less than extraordinary, both in their voices and in their lives! We've created a way to integrate cutting edge processes of vocal unfolding with personal development tools of the highest calibre.

"Archetype: 1. The original pattern or model after which a thing is made; a model or first form; prototype. 2. (In Jungian psychology) an unconscious idea, pattern of thought, image, etc, inherited from the ancestors of the race and universally present in individual psyches."

Our 10-pound Random House Dictionary of the English Language defines the concept of archetype in this way: "Archetype: 1. The original pattern or model after which a thing is made; a model or first form; prototype. 2. (In Jungian psychology) an unconscious idea, pattern of thought, image, etc, inherited from the ancestors of the race and universally present in individual psyches."

Whenever something is true for all people, there are immutable principles at work, principles that hold true across race and culture, time and space. We have discovered the principles of this fascinating inner world and have come up with our own rather expanded definition of Archetype. We have come to call them 'Living Archetypes' to emphasize the fact that they are alive inside each one of us, evolving, learning and responding, and not just some static, collected ideas printed in a book. Within every human being is a Warrior, Magician, Lover and Sovereign whose energy and internal dynamics is a perfect expression of our uniqueness.

- Living Archetype: One of the four primordial pillars of the individual psyche universally present, though personally unique, in all human beings as our own Sovereign, Lover, Magician, and Warrior.

- These Living Archetypes are naturally present in our neurophysiology as the personifications of the four primordial energies of Sovereign (Being), Lover (Feeling), Magician (Thinking), and Warrior (Doing).

- Each of these four Living Archetypes has two aspects - male and female; in other words, each of us has within us both a male and a female Sovereign, Lover, Magician, and Warrior.

- These Living Archetypes are intent upon the highest growth of the individual towards our highest potential.

- Each of the four Living Archetypes is intent upon connection with the other three.

- These Living Archetypes function below the surface of the conscious mind, though their real and dynamic world can be easily and consciously entered into.

- This Living Archetypal world can be reordered with our conscious attention, intention, focus, and action.

- Changes in the inner world of the Living Archetypes naturally result in changes in our conscious outside world.

- All our Being, Feeling, Thinking and Doing in the arena of the conscious mind and its outward activities is a summation of the decisions, feelings, attitudes, and activities that have first been formed in the personal realm of the Living Archetypes.

- The world of the Living Archetypes has always been here waiting for us to discover and use in the transformation of our lives towards our greatest potential, as a tool and a touchstone for humanity.

Lots of people have brought to our attention that in the world of literature there seem to be many, many archetypes. We believe they can all be distilled down to Sovereign, Lover, Magician and Warrior. This model of the Four Living Archetypes is complete because together they encompass all the areas of our human life: Being, Feeling, Thinking and Doing, and this equals Sovereign, Lover, Magician and, Warrior.

The Sovereign is our unique individual Being, the wholeness of our self. The Lover is our Feeling self, the Magician is our Thinking self, and the Warrior is our Doing self.

Each of the Living Archetypes has an inner and an outer aspect. The Sovereign encompasses the outer physical wholeness of who we are as more than the sum of our different parts. The Sovereign also guides our spiritual destiny, that inner sense of the direction of our life. The Lover encompasses both our outer physical sensory system and our inner capacity to feel and know emotion. The Magician encompasses both our outer physical information processing systems and our inner creative, intuitive, and everyday thinking. The Warrior encompasses both our outer physical motor systems and our inner ability to perform action, to get things done.

We hope you're getting the idea that the four primordial Living Archetypes, called Sovereign, Lover, Magician, and Warrior are more than just ideas. They are more than just stories from the mists of time. They are more than just pictures in a book or sculptures from antiquity. The four foundational Living Archetypes are very much alive inside each of us, and are extremely practical tools for our lives of the most intensely personal nature. They are the voices of the soul, they are the agents of the soul, they create our lives, and they can tell our stories and sing our songs.

*"Look within.
Within is the fountain
of good, and it will ever
bubble up, if thou wilt
ever dig."*

Author: Marcus Aurelius,
Roman emperor, AD 121-180

Chapter 8

The Sovereign, The Lover, The Magician and The Warrior

Chapter 8

The Sovereign, The Lover, The Magician and The Warrior

Before we go any further, let's describe each of the Living Archetypes and their attributes:

Sovereign - I Am

When you are born, you are unique, and that feeling of uniqueness stays with you for life. This uniqueness is the manifestation of the Sovereign, the subtlest level of the individual personality that always feels the same no matter what happens or how much time passes. It is the essence of your identity. We feel it could be said that the prime directive of the Sovereign is to profoundly know your innermost nature and to bring your unique energy and talents out into the world.

Up until the mid-teen years, the Sovereign could be said to be in training; in particular, learning by example from our mothers, fathers, and others close to us, about how to be the King and Queen of our own life. We are starting to get a picture, a feeling of how we want to run our life. Or not run it.

All going well, by the mid-teen years your Sovereign energy has naturally matured to the point where you have the desire to start to take responsibility for yourself, for your choices and for your decisions. A few years pass and you naturally expand further outward. You realize that you need to be in a relationship with the world, too, perhaps realizing with a shock that it's not all about you anymore! As the Sovereign energy matures during your lifetime, your circle of influence and responsibility extends, radiating outwards to your family, your environment, your community, your nation, and your world. The unfolding of the Sovereign energy over your lifetime is one of bringing the indefinable uniqueness of who you are out into the world and making the world a better and more interesting place because of it.

On the day-to-day level of your internal functioning, the role of your Sovereign is more in keeping with the traditional definition of King and Queen. Your Sovereign is responsible for inspiring, guiding, unifying, ordering, and deciding. Your Sovereign is responsible for unifying the relationship between that innermost unique Sovereign aspect of yourself and your internal worlds of feeling (Lover), thinking (Magician), and doing (Warrior). In other words, your Sovereign must always know what's going on in your inner kingdom. And, if this is happens, the essence of who you are deep inside will continuously translate into your outer life, and you will always be growing in the flow of your life's purpose.

Some occupations associated with the Sovereign are: Kings and Queens, Tribal Chieftains, Presidents, CEOs, Ship Captains, and leaders of any type of organization.

One of Edwin's favourite cases comes from a gentleman attending a weekend event.

Edwin: *"His history was as a successful businessman but he would change jobs frequently. He physically worked out but had had lower back pain for over 15 years and could not easily sit on the floor with his legs crossed.*

During the process of relocating and integrating his Living Archetypes we discovered his Magician, huge in size, very smart and sitting up in his head on a throne. Unfortunately this is a fairly common scenario in our culture. In this case, as in most cases, the Magician had not tried to usurp the King's power, but was trying to 'fill in' because the King was not there, as we'll see. I asked him where his King was and he said that he was five years old on a swing in his back yard. I asked what happened when he was five, and he said his father died.

His Sovereign had become, you could say, frozen in time. During a simple process we exchanged the positions of the Magician and the Sovereign. The spirit of his father actually came to show the King his throne.

The next day he looked so good I barely recognized him! I asked him what had happened last night. He said, 'My king has grown up!' Plus, the man's back pain had disappeared and he could cross his legs for the first time in years.

It was such an instant change and a deep insight into his life; such a powerful shift! It came about so effortlessly and gracefully it was truly amazing. The whole process took about 10 minutes. It's not easy to express to you the power of this work and the remarkable voices and music that come from it."

Another client who owned a business with approximately 30 employees had a session with Edwin that illuminates the power of the Living Archetypes to give deep insights into life on many levels.

Edwin: *"While looking for his Sovereign during a session, I was suddenly inspired to ask him, 'When you're with your family, how is your King?' He answered, 'It's like Shangri-La. Waterfalls, children playing, happiness.' Then I asked, 'How is your King when you are at work?' He said, 'The King is in a dark room without windows."*

The following is what unfolded from this dramatic insight. He explained that his business was highly competitive. The general rule that guided everyone was to make as much money as possible in as little time as possible, so one could then be able to create and live another life with your family, or do whatever else you dreamed.

My instinct was that you cannot separate family and business, and that is clearly what had happened in his business, and in fact most modern business. I suggested one simple thing. That he treat the members of his business as if they were family. Prior to this he was mostly just concerned with paying them and bidding successfully on every contract that he went for. His life was stressful, his success rate about 40% and there was no real joy and connection in the business. He came home for this. He was also very nervous giving his business presentations and bids. There was so much pressure on him.

Following my suggestion and stepping into his King energy, rather than running on his Magician energy, the results were significant. In the following year, his company doubled in size and he won every single contract he bid on, even against major competition that underbid him. He also felt much more at ease giving his presentations. He also gained the attention of key people in the industry. Clearly he'd stepped into his Sovereignty."

The Living Archetypes completely reflected the imbalance of his life and showed up a societal imbalance as well. We have given businesses a life of their own that can rule us instead of serving us. We've created businesses and corporations to be separate legal entities, concerned primarily with the bottom line of profit and survival. We have given them power and laws of their own that do not necessarily sustain and serve humanity. It seems to be an unsustainable model that can certainly take the joy out of living and interacting together as a community.

This is an example of the sorts of profound insights that come from this work with the Living Archetypes. This is the level that you need to be at to write a great song and express yourself in a voice that is fully congruent.

An example of a Sovereign song: 'Let It Be" by the Beatles.

Lover - I Feel

When you were born, your senses were wide open and your emotions were without inhibition, everything was a sea of sensation and feeling. Your needs were the only ones, and, of all of them, the needs for love, touch, and connection were the greatest. There is no clearer manifestation of the qualities of the Living Archetype of the Lover than when you were an infant. When you were happy you smiled, when you were hungry you cried, when you were tired, you slept, and when you needed something you had an inherent trust that it would be provided. The Lover feels everything, simultaneously feeling both every physical sensation in the body itself and also the constantly flowing inner tides of emotion. The Lover is profoundly connected to the power of Love in the universe; it could be said that the Lover is that power focused and individualized. It seems that the Lover has an infinite capacity to feel. Inside the body, the Lover functions through the sensory system, riding the tides of sensation and emotion. The Lover's ability to feel is not confined to the individual body; the Lover is also capable of unerringly picking up on what others are feeling as well. In fact, they can feel almost anything they put their attention on – a picture of someone in a magazine, animals, plants, etc. The Lover always seeks to feel good, and a large measure of human activity is driven by this basic need.

The Lover longs to always feel content and good in the body, and longs to have the senses filled with varied objects of enjoyment. The Lover wishes to fill the ears with a symphony of sounds, to fill the eyes with beauty and variety. The Lover wishes to fully feel textures and temperatures against the skin. The Lover wishes to smell all the layers of all the smells of all the flowers in the world. The Lover wants to taste the most delicious tastes. The Lover also wishes to feel himself in relation to the sensory input coming in from outside; that is, to hear himself –how does he sound? To touch himself – how does he feel? To see himself - how does he look? To taste his own saliva - what is that like? To smell himself - what is that current of scent drifting through the air today? The world is an endless exploration for the senses, and, for that, the Lover's quest is life long.

On the day-to-day functioning level, the Lover experiences the senses and emotions. Are you too hot, too cold, hungry, or tired? Are you sad, angry, amused or joyful? All this input is extremely valuable information, which is directly connected to our survival and happiness. The Lover is driven to seek out that which makes you feel better. The Lover longs to express and experience beauty. The Lover is driven to connect with others to express and experience love. The Lover connects with the natural world and the cosmos to feel that glorious expansion and intimacy with creation itself. With this, the Lover reaffirms that, yes, you are profoundly, deeply connected with the mystery of life.

Some occupations associated with the Lover are: Artists, musicians, poets, naturalists, chefs, fashion designers, aroma therapists, massage therapists, sommeliers, and all occupations in the helping and healing fields.

A woman who owns a coaching training business had a session with Edwin:

Edwin: *"My instincts told me that the Lovers were not so involved. I asked her how her Lovers were. She said the Male and Female Lovers were in her heart together and very happy. I asked her how old they were, and she said they were seventeen years old. She was currently around forty years old. Her Lovers had never grown up. She had fallen in love with her high school sweetheart, married him, and created a kind of time capsule, so that things could never change and they could be in love forever.*

People generally misunderstand the importance of the Lover energy in business. Her Lovers were still in that first stage of being in love where you don't even know anyone else exists. It's a natural stage but an immature stage. The Lover energy is meant to grow and evolve from the inside out. From loving yourself to the one you love, to your family and friends, to the people you work with, to your customers, to your society, to your country and to the world, the universe, and beyond! This is how we grow. This is how the Lover energy expands in the world. Businesses succeed not just through the actions of the Warrior and the skills of the Magician, and the vision of the Sovereign. The Lover is very important as the sales force in a company, connecting with others. Her Lovers were not active in the outside world, and that is why even with everything else in place her company was no longer growing.

I suggested that her Lovers love the people of her country. She immediately felt a great pain as she felt their struggles and challenges. But now she also knew what they needed. As the pain lifted, her Lovers started to grow up, to mature, and new creative ideas began to flow that would bring her the business she wanted.

Again, the Living Archetypes gave the deep understanding needed for real results. Through the integration of movement, sound, singing, song, and the Living Archetypes, she healed her isolated Lovers and was able to begin to expand her love to all."

Edwin once did a session with a policeman who worked in a high-crime district.

Edwin: *"His main concern was his relationship with his wife. Because of his occupation, he was trained not to bring personal feelings into work. The problem was that he was continuing to do the same at home with his wife. He was not able to feel emotions at home. So he was not able to feel his love for his wife or feel what his wife needed either. It's no wonder his relationship with his wife was cold and they were considering a divorce when he came to the private session.*

He was not a big man at all but he had a very strong Male warrior. Indeed, as a policeman his Warriors were trained to be strong and not to feel anything. We did an integration process with his Warrior energy and figured out a way he could take off his armour when he came home.

We found that his main imbalance was in the Lovers. The Male and Female were apart and there was a lot of sadness, pain and numbness. Bringing them together was remarkable; they fell in love again. His whole persona changed as he softened, relaxed, and became himself. He was able to feel love again. As far as we know, he and his wife are still together!"

Through the work with the Living Archetypes, we can see that our educational model provides mostly an education for the Magician and Warrior. The Lover education is minimal, if any, seemingly limited to information about birth control. We are not taught how to deeply connect with others and develop and nurture love over time. It is obvious by the sheer number of divorces in these days that our Lovers are in trouble. Lovers need time together to grow, and our busy world today does not encourage this.

An example of a Lover song: "Something (In the Way She Moves)" by the Beatles.

The Magician – I Think

Soon after you are born, your Magician starts to figure out how things work in this world. You started with simple things like distinguishing dark and light shapes, and distinguishing your mother's voice. You moved on to figuring out how to roll over, how to walk and how to talk. Your Magician was so relieved to begin to talk so you could finally ask 'WHY?' Every parent is both delighted and exasperated by the hundreds, by the thousands of 'whys' of their child's Magician, ranging from topics whimsical to profound. The Magician wants to know everything, and the brain itself must grow to support this. It is well known that the numbers of new neurological connections being created in a young child are far greater than at any other time in our lives. When the brain physiology has matured toward it's adult size, sometime in the teenage years, the Magician becomes capable of abstract thought - what if..?

The Magician's energy is the flow of processing and analyzing information. The Magician is associated with the intellect; it's the part of us that draws distinctions and figures out how things work. It's the part of us that solves problems, the part of us that can focus on something, copy it, learn it, and improve upon it. The Magician takes information and puts it together in different ways. He experiments with solutions. The Magician is creative and intuitive, seeming to pull solutions out of the air, capable of bridging the gap between two seeming impossibilities. The Magician's ability to expand is infinite as there's always something else to learn! The Magician wants to understand the meaning of life, and explore its endless possibilities.

On the day-to-day functioning level, the Magician represents the skills we have learned, our jobs and all other areas of specialized knowledge. If you are a student, very likely you are exercising your Magician strenuously - reading, remembering, retrieving, ordering, re-forming, synthesizing, and hypothesizing information to somehow achieve the passing grade.

Firstly, up until the teenage years, the Magician is driven to know the basic skills and information for living. Then, during the teen years, the time of the maturing of the brain physiology, the Magician becomes driven to understand all about himself, who he is, his uniqueness. He is driven to explore possibilities of how he can fit into the world around him and how he can best utilize his natural tendencies and talents.

Some occupations associated with the Magician are: Anything to do with computers and technology, invention, teaching, diplomacy, the entrepreneurial,; the academic, researching, translating, technical writing, the law, bureaucracy, the stock market, marketing, and advertising, and politics.

Cheryl*: "I was working with a young man named Kentaro from Japan through an interpreter. I was guiding him to find and connect with his various archetypes. He was in such visible pain it seemed that the state of the Lover would be central to this session. It didn't turn out that way. It turned out that the pain was in the Magician, so much so that he had considered suicide several times.*

It turned out that his entire educational experience had been incredibly stressful; he was not good at school and had many experiences of failure. He had immense pressure from home to succeed. He ended up going to University on the basis of that pressure and again met with many failures. He tried with his whole being to succeed, and at best got mediocre marks. He ended up in a job that he does not like.

It was obvious to me that he wasn't cut out to be an academic, and had been forced by family and society to take that road.

The session focused on bringing the Male and Female Magicians together. Kentaro indicated that they were so beaten down they had no hope left. They had no belief in themselves that they had the potential to learn anything to the degree that other people seemed to learn. They were at the end of their rope.

In the process of bringing them together, they started to release the incredible amount of stress that their educational experience and societal expectations had given them. They started to gain an understanding of what they'd been through in the bigger picture. Tentatively they connected, and they were able to come to the place where they were starting to consider some new options and possibilities.

This man, like many other people, experienced so much suffering in a purely academic environment. I find it a tragedy he couldn't be supported to find and pursue his own style of learning when he was young."

Kentarto is one of our 6-Day Japanese language Tofino graduates, and Miwa Kashu, the heart and soul of our business in Japan, received this message from him several months afterwards:

"Today, I took the courage to listen to my recorded song for the first time.

My singing voice was far more beautiful that I thought it would be.

I was so fearful to listen to it that it had been kept in a closet.

Your email has helped me to realize how fearful I had been to face my true self.

I want to thank you. See you again."

"Today, I took the courage to listen to my recorded song for the first time.

My singing voice was far more beautiful that I thought it would be.

I was so fearful to listen to it that it had been kept in a closet.

Your email has helped me to realize how fearful I had been to face my true self.

I want to thank you. See you again."

He's in the process of re-ordering his world, from the inside out!

An example of a Magician Song: "I am the Walrus" by the Beatles.

The Warrior - I Act

From the moment you were born your Warrior was engaged in mastering your physical body. The development of the necessary coordination of life takes a lot of dedicated playing - it can take, for example, six years or so to learn to catch a ball, or ride a bicycle. The young Warrior doesn't care how many hundreds of times he fails or hurts himself in the process; he picks himself up for another attempt. He is driven to succeed.

While in the initial stages of speaking, the Warrior learns a very useful word, 'NO!' which is closely related to 'MINE!' which follows soon after. These are the first words of the Warrior. Before this time, in the time of babyhood, the infant floats in the love and care of his family, needing and desiring nothing else. But with mobility and speech, it becomes obvious and necessary for each one of us to assert our rights of personhood. The Warrior performs this task for us. The first right of personhood is choice, or the power to decide for ourselves what we do or do not prefer, and what we will or will not allow. The second right of personhood is space, or a place that is mine alone, and this includes the things I choose to put in that space. With these natural developments, the little Warrior in us puts all his considerable passion into asserting his desire and ability to choose by defending his right to deny - NO! and defending what is his - MINE!

This time period is traditionally known as the 'terrible twos', but we think it only can become terrible when parents try and fight natural child development. In the long run, we as parents will make things difficult for our child's Warrior by not allowing the child to make any choices that affect him or her, and by forcing him or her to 'share' before ready to. These assertions of personhood - choice, and standing up for ourselves - are, in the end, essential survival tools that we all need to have sharp to survive well, and for our genes to survive into the future, which after all seems to be the goal of all life on Earth.

The Warrior is concerned with physical survival and instinct. When the Warrior reaches the teenage years and the body starts to mature sexually, his attention is naturally drawn more and more to that most fascinating subject – reproduction of the species. The Warrior's competitive nature starts to get more serious, and what may start as a friendly get together can turn very intense as everyone fights to get the best, most desirable mate. Again, survival, as the choice and winning of a mate can mean the difference between success and failure, between misery and happiness, between loneliness and status, and perhaps even the difference between life and death. The Warrior does his best to make himself as physically attractive as possible, being completely tuned into physical chemistry and body attraction. Anything to do with being physical engages the Warrior, and that includes the discipline, and the mental muscles, that are required to keep the body in good running order. As the Warrior matures in life, he starts to notice that many other Warriors are not as strong as he is, so he naturally begins to look out for others, look out for those that can't protect or take care of themselves, and he steps up. He gets deep satisfaction out of service to others, and the credo of the Warrior could very well be 'To Serve and Protect'.

In day-to-day life our Warrior creates our daily routine and tries to stick to it, even when it requires some sacrifice of him. Structure and order are vital to him, and he likes to have a place for everything and everything in its place. He acts to fulfil our needs and desires. Hungry? He will find you some food. Bored? He will go out late at night to rent a movie. Threatened? He will stand up and fight to the death if necessary. Anything you want, the Warrior will do his best to do it for you. He's the one who will run on empty in order to make a deadline. He's the one who feels a threat, small or large, and guards against it. He's the one who makes you get up to go to aerobics class when you don't want to.

Some occupations associated with the Warrior are: Anything to do with sports, the physical trades – carpenters, plumbers, fabricators - anyone who works with his hands for a living; also, the Police and the Armed Forces.

Cheryl: *"The Warrior is always affected by whatever happens to our bodies. I did a session recently with Uyo from Japan. She had been bothered by asthma since she was a child. When she found her Male Warrior he was smoking. Her father used to smoke when she was a child, and her mother was often angry with him for not quitting even though Uyo had asthma. The Warrior was showing Uyo the influence her father's smoking still had on her physical condition of asthma. She was still holding that influence in her body."*

Cheryl: *"Years ago, I did a general session with a lovely singer,*

TT from Canada. She was open about her struggles with alcohol and is an active member of AA. She had been sober for 8 or 9 years. We were going through her Living Archetypes, and when we came to the Warriors, we discovered that the Male Warrior was still drinking. To her this was a 'eureka moment' because she still found it very difficult to stay away from alcohol. At last she was able to understand where this strong pull to drink came from. This story illustrates the power of any physical habit. Even though there wasn't an emotional desire for alcohol anymore, the physical habit was very hard for TT to resist."

Edwin: *"I once was asked to give a session to one of the top men in an international company. On meeting him in the lunch line and suggesting a session with his voice, he said, 'I've had a weak voice for many years.' I said, 'When did this happen?' He said, 'I was playing American football in college and I got a full elbow in my throat. I was not able to make any sound for three months.' I replied, 'Dude, your Warrior was taken out!'*

When we were going through his Living Archetypes, we came to the male Warrior. We found the Warrior to be a cardboard cut out about 10 feet in front of him, put there by the Magician so that at least he appeared to have a Warrior. Clearly his Warrior had been taken out. Interestingly enough, his wife was at this event, and it was clear to me she was acting in the capacity of his Warrior. She was bigger than he was and seemed to me quite dominating; it didn't seem to be a happy relationship. The process we chose was to move his Warrior energy to his chest. The Warrior instantly began to wake up and become stronger, and his voice also dramatically improved.

A month or so later, I attempted to connect with him at his place of work and was told that he'd quit his job, left his wife, and nobody knew where he was! Clearly, his Warrior had woken up and taken action."

An example of a Warrior song: "Hard Day's Night" by the Beatles.

The next evolution of our archetypal journey came about by a serendipitous accident.

Cheryl*: "I found I could actually see into the realm of the Living Archetypes. It happened one night as I was focusing with Edwin on his own internal archetypal world. Suddenly it appeared in my mind's eye in living colour, just like a movie with the archetypes themselves as the living players. The archetypes appeared one by one, spoke, moved, and used body language to communicate. Consequently, I found understanding this brand new world was extremely easy. I could hear the Living Archetype's direct* *statements and I could interact with them. I could see their body language and pick up additional clues from their environment. As I went through this process it readily became apparent that the world of the Living Archetypes is not static but alive, highly dynamic and fluid. It reacts to input, grows and changes, and receives insight right before the eyes. I was immediately amazed with how transparent the Living Archetypes were in terms of emotion, appearance and clarity of communication. It was impossible to miss how their body language, appearance, and words reflected their state of mind, and how easy it was to tell what they were feeling. I was amazed at how they responded to questions with such honesty and candor. I was also amazed at how they could change so fast."*

Up until this time, we weren't entirely certain that the world of the Living Archetypes wasn't just metaphoric and symbolic rather than "really" real. We still weren't one hundred percent certain that their existence wasn't more than just distinct, physical energies in the body. We weren't one hundred percent sure that their existence wasn't more than a creation of the intellect on some level of wishful imagination. The clear, undeniable reality of the Living Archetypal realm came as a revelation, but one that has been made irrefutable over time by the personal insights and the results of thousands of peoples' experiences.

How can this world exist under our very noses without our being consciously aware of it? The Living Archetypal world functions on a level below the surface of the conscious mind. We don't know why. It is a magnificent mystery within our neurophysiology that we both hope will be scientifically unlocked during our lifetimes.

Given the right direction, we have found that quite a large percentage of people can see into their own Living Archetypal world the same way Cheryl can. Everyone's connection to their own perception is somewhat unique. Some people begin by being able to feel and see the world of the Living Archetypes clearly right off the bat. With some others, this ability develops over time. Some people feel rather than see their internal landscape, sensing energy shifts and emotion. Some people only hear what the Living Archetypes are saying. Some people see shifting colours along with sensing the specific Living Archetypal emotional climate. It depends upon the person. As long as someone can internally distinguish between the different Living Archetypal energies, and as long as they can receive some distinct impression in return, communication is established with the specific Living Archetypal energies, and a dialogue, and thus transformation, is guaranteed. None of the thousands of people who have crossed our path over the years, who have experienced the various courses we have offered, have been unable to get a sense of the energies of the Living Archetypes. It never fails; everyone can easily access this world of the Living Archetypes and be positively impacted by the connection.

We work with the Living Archetypes in different yet complementary ways. Edwin usually works more with the integration of the Living Archetypes, sound and song. He uses the Living Archetypes to focus a song, to find out what it is really about, to get the ultimate value from it. They are what he calls an advanced vocal technique that naturally creates the perfect tone to carry the message of the song. Edwin describes the Living Archetypes as the ultimate vocal technique because they bring the subtlest level of the mind/body energy alive in the voice. For us, the song's ultimate value is both in terms of its visceral, long-lasting transformational impact on the person who wrote it, and also in the actual vocal recording of it. Recorded, the song can continue to act and inspire, expressing a story and creating a precise sequence of resonances that can affect others in the same way.

Edwin: *"A client, RH from the USA, had written a song, the chorus of which went: 'Where are all the heroes, I've been so long without one.' I'd worked with RH for some time; his poetry was exquisite, but he had never really been able to consistently sing in tune. Exploring this song, we discovered that his Warrior had written the song to his father. It made complete sense; his father was in the Army and was rarely home. So RH's Warrior never had a hero to follow, never had anyone to model. A young boy loves and needs to model his father. I had him sing from his Warrior to his father, and it worked like magic. The pain of the disconnection between his Warrior and his father came up and began to heal as he sang the song, and, for the first time, he consistently sang in tune with a powerful congruent tone.*

The technology of the Living Archetypes is breathtaking in its ability to heal people's lives from the inside out. But to me it is also an unprecedented technology for working with the voice."

Cheryl usually works with non-music individual sessions with the Living Archetypes. Her expertise is guiding people through their own internal Living Archetypal landscape. She helps people to find and communicate with their own Living Archetypes, often revolving around a specific topic.

There are many wonderful examples, ancient and modern, that remind us of the wholeness of the four-fold modality. Coming down from ancient times, and still alive today, the enormous amount of information originally cognized by ancient seers and collectively known as the Veda (Sanskrit for 'knowledge') has been passed on in oral traditions that have spanned thousands of years. It's a vast living storehouse of spiritual and practical knowledge having all its roots in, you guessed it, the 4 primary Vedas: Rig Veda, Sama Veda, Yajur Veda, and Atharva Veda.

From our understanding, the functioning of these four Vedas corresponds exactly with the energies of the Sovereign, Lover, Magician and Warrior, respectively. According to some Vedic scholars, all knowledge - past, present and future, has its roots in one of these four Vedas. It seems to us there is a direct correlation between the nature and functioning of these four Vedas and the nature and function of the four Living Archetypes deep within us.

Another example: Edwin is fond of seeing the Fab Four - The Beatles - in context of the Living Archetypes as well. Sir Paul McCartney, writer of 'Let it Be' and knighted by the Queen of England, embodies the Sovereign quality. George Harrison, the writer of 'While my Guitar Gently Weeps' and 'Something in the Way She Moves', embodies the Lover quality. His guitar playing was not the heavy metal Warrior or the super-technical Magician. He played beautiful melodic 'fills' that brought everything together. John Lennon, writer of 'I am the Walrus' and other wildly creative lyrics, embodies the Magician quality. Ringo Starr, with his solid beat holding down the groove, embodies the Warrior quality. He kept the structure solid so everyone knew where they were. No one can deny that together these four men made one heck of a band! One could easily argue that they were instrumental in changing the world. Talk about lasting impact!

We think that 'The Four Agreements', a book by Don Miguel Ruiz, published by Amber-Allen, also perfectly illustrates the

Living Archetypal model. Its central philosophy is based on the integrity of four different elements:

'Be impeccable with your word.' For us, this represents the Sovereign energy in integrity.

'Don't take anything personally.' For us, this represents the Lover energy in integrity.

'Don't make assumptions.' For us, this represents the Magician energy in integrity.

'Always do your best.' For us, this represents the Warrior energy in integrity. This book has had enormous success. We believe this is because it illustrates the universal principles of the Living Archetypes, and attempts to bring them into balance.

For Sci-Fi fans, consider Star Trek - the Next Generation as another example. The functions and qualities of the main characters, from the bridge of the star ship Enterprise, coincide perfectly with the 4 - fold archetypal model. Jean-Luc Picard, the captain of the Enterprise, represents the Sovereign energy in a very high integrity. Deanna Troy, counsellor and empath from another planet, represents the Lover energy. Data, the android, in control of all things technical, represents the Magician energy. Worf, an alien from a planet of warriors, in control of all security matters, represents the Warrior energy. Commander Riker, second in command, embodies Sovereign-in-training, which you could say is the position of all of us. We are all learning to be the captain of our own spaceship, the master of our own destiny. These Enterprise crewmembers have a loyalty and interdependence that seems to be invincible. We long for this kind of order inside. The Star Trek series, introduced in the 1960s and reintroduced in the 1980s, is still alive today in re-runs, spin-offs and sequels. We believe its global popularity comes from the creators managing to create their stories around this underlying order that is basic to human functioning. When we have all these Living Archetypal energies strong and working together we, too, can succeed '… in boldly going where no one has gone before!...' Someone could write a Ph.D. paper on it!

Yet another example: Think even about the structure of a newspaper. Newspapers devote different sections to satisfy the needs of the different Living Archetypes within us. Global News of the world, or the front-page news would fall under Sovereign interest. Arts/Entertainment/Home/Life/ Gardening/ Food news would fall under Lover interest. Stock Market, Business, Classifieds, Crossword, Comics, Advertising, and Financial news falls under the interest of the Magician. Sports news falls under the interest of the Warrior. If any of these sections were missing, the paper would feel incomplete.

How about: Looking for the energy of each of the Living Archetypes in your life:

Your Warrior: the strength of your physical life force, your level of fitness, your ability to act, your self-discipline, your ability to sacrifice for the greater good.

Your Magician: your ability to master any skill, your creativity, your adaptability, your ability to problem solve.

Your Lover: your level of happiness, your level of connectedness to others, nature, and the cosmos.

Your Sovereign: your vision for your life, and your moral and ethical functioning levels.

"Do not commit your poems to pages alone, sing them I pray you."

Virgil, Ancient Roman poet 70 BC -19 BC

Conclusion

Conclusion

Singing is an essential activity for a human being! No matter how much music we may listen to, if we do not sing we are unfulfilled and unexpressed on some level. The longer we do not sing in our lives, the heavier grows the weight within us. We see this constantly everywhere we go, even if people are unaware of it themselves. When they finally get the opportunity to express their natural voice it's as if a huge weight is lifted from them. Their faces change, their body language changes, their energy level goes up, they smile with relief; the lights come back on!

So why do we believe singing is an essential activity for a human being?

Principle: In addition to our being inwardly connected to ourselves, we are also meant to be fully expressed in the outside world. We believe this is a universal requirement of human nature and human need: to bring our unique inner self outward and interface this expression with the world around us. It is not enough to know ourselves inside; we must express it outside as well. The voice is your most direct means to express yourself.

Principle: You must learn to experience and sing in the field of unbounded emotional energy. This is a unique and specific experience. Singing in this way, you can fully feel, fully express, and fully convey that huge fullness of all that you are feeling. Singing with the power of unbounded emotional energy you can finally realize the enormous natural healing potential of your emotions. We have become convinced that singing is the only way to experience this field of unbounded emotional energy and bring it into our lives! Humanity has forgotten how, and we have become separated from our own emotions and separated from the energy of nature. Our very happiness and identity as a human being has been lost, and singing is critical in order to regain it. We've all been crippled without the experience of the field of unbounded emotional energy.

Principle: You must write your own songs! Songs tell our story as individuals, and as a people existing in a certain time. It is a record of our feeling and thinking and history. Our culture is one of the iPod filled with songs. Everywhere you go today people are plugged in, walking down the street, on the bus, at home, at school, and as the background to any task. They have an insatiable appetite to be surrounded by song and can't seem to get enough. This is the power of songs. What if we all wrote our own songs? It is so important to do so, because nobody, no matter how talented they are, can express who we are and our place in time and space except us. Wouldn't it be a beautiful thing if every family had a legacy of songs written by members of the family that were passed on and added to every generation?

Principle: You must sing your own songs! The magical effects of a song lie in the combination of the story of the song with the generated tones of the melody. Together they create a powerful, unfathomable effect as they resonate through the bodies and the psyches of anyone who listens to them. Our son played the cello for some time when he was young and when he practiced, the floor would vibrate, the table would vibrate, we could even feel our bones vibrate. It's the same thing with singing. When your real sound comes out, it vibrates through your physiology from the inside out as it finds its own way. This sequence of vibration is unconsciously, naturally created by a person to express the emotion of their own story, and it coincidently ends up creating health and healing for themselves, body and soul. This vibration, this powerful resonance of a song, wakes you up inside and reminds you what you really sound like, whom this person really is, the real quality of your energy, your personality, and your presence. The actual physical vibration is key.

Principle: Your songs create expression, understanding and healing in the inner world of your Living Archetypes! It is crucial to experience your Living Archetypes to understand and bring balance to all aspects, and between all aspects of your life. It is vital to energize and balance your Being, Feeling, Thinking and Doing so you'll live on the highest level of functioning. It is impossible to create this balance from the level of your conscious mind. Fortunately you have within, naturally built into your humanness, the realm of the Living Archetypes existing below the level of the conscious mind. With the proper focus and attention it's simple to begin to create balance inside. It's a simple, visceral, fascinating experience to voyage within the realm of the Living Archetypes.

Edwin: *"Since the course I took on the Archetypes in the 1990s, neither Cheryl nor I have studied any other literature on the Archetypes, or taken any other seminars of that nature. We'd rather have the Living Archetypes tell us themselves! And they have, in great detail, through our seminars and sessions over the years. On our courses, people get in touch with their own Living Archetypes and write songs from them and about them. Sharing through thousands of songs and sessions is how we have continued to learn about this inner world. Songs are so amazing in their power to reveal the truth, and to set truth on its purifying course through your body, your mind, your emotions and your soul. The truth will indeed set you free!"*

Ultimately, your Sovereign captain carries the inner knowingness of where he's going, the Lover experiences each moment of the journey and keeps the connection of love between members of the crew so they have the heart to keep going, the Magician charts the actual compass course given to him by the Sovereign, and the Warrior physically steers the boat according to the charted course, hoists and mends the sails, and swabs the deck. You can see that without one or the other of the Living Archetypes strong and present, your ship of life can become lost at sea. Time passes. Your whole lifetime can pass you by. In awakening to the inner world of the Living Archetypes and bringing them together, their togetherness, their wholeness, creates a specific physical experience, a synergy, which is something more than the sum of the parts. It's this synergy in the moment, this inner vitality that's tapped, that strengthens and brings understanding, dimension, and flow to the magic of your life's purpose. And so, your journey of life keeps unfolding with dignity, power, grace, joy and fun!

Put it into song! There are so many of your songs that need to be heard! Songs pulled from somewhere deep inside. Songs that tell our story. Songs that make us laugh! Songs that are completely surprising. Songs that move to tears. Songs that rend the fibres of pain. Songs that express the sacredness of life. Songs that soothe like the sea on a calm day. We all have this capacity within us!

Have your family start to create a legacy of songs! Songs that are passed on and added to every generation. Songs that become associated with certain times of the year. Songs that continue to be sung even though the singer has grown up or passed on. Songs that come to symbolize the essence of who you are as a family.

We feel proud and joyful to be participating in a renaissance of real humanity. What do we mean by that? We want to help create a world where the Unbounded Voice is alive in everyone! We want to help create a world where everyone has a voice. A world where the intrinsic natural beauty of each voice can and will really be heard. A world where it is natural for everyone to write and sing the songs that come from deep inside. A world where there is safety, connection, respect and appreciation for the singer and where they've been. A world where we all know we belong - in our families, in our communities, in our countries, and of course, on our dear spinning world hurtling through space!

Everyone singing their own songs from the heart can help create a wonderful world! Imagine yourself in the circle of your family and friends singing your songs! Imagine a world resonating with tens, with hundreds, with thousands, with millions, with billions of voices and their songs, telling and celebrating the unfolding story of humanity!

The last 30 years of Edwin's life have unfolded from his asking the question, 'How do you sing?' We now believe we do know! We all sing by freeing the physiology, freeing the psyche and singing through the field of unbounded emotional energy.

Join us with your Unbounded Voice to Wake Up and Sing!

"The only thing better than singing is more singing."

Ella Fitzgerald,
American Jazz singer 1917-1996

More Songs and Stories

More Songs and Stories

UMBRELLAS, UMBRELLAS by Jill Chivers

This song became alive when Edwin asked me at Tofino, "What is the most feminine thing you can think of?" and I said, "Umbrellas." He responded, "Umbrellas?????" And I said, "Yes, you know, like a Mary Poppins- type umbrella that could lift you off into somewhere else, into a different world."

My focus in life tends to be about bringing balance to my feminine side and being grounded and centred.

Working or playing with the archetypes both female and male inside of myself in the way Edwin and Cheryl do it helps me to accomplish this better internal balance. Through this song it also showed me how I like to escape into other worlds, hence the challenge to stay grounded and centred.

Through this 'Umbrellas, Umbrellas' song, which is a very playful uplifting song, I found my feminine archetypes talking to my masculine archetypes, sending the message to lighten up, and play and be free to enjoy life. It worked. When I sang the song I twirled a BIG umbrella round and round, and was in a state of joyfulness and playfulness. I felt uplifted by my own song and felt internally full of delight.

UMBRELLAS

Umbrellas, umbrellas
Be open to it fellas
Umbrellas, umbrellas
Be open to it fellas

Such a feminine thing
Can be used as a wing
To escape this world
Just needs to be twirled
And you're in another world

Umbrellas, umbrellas
Be open to it fellas
Umbrellas, umbrellas
Be open to it fellas

Pink, purple and yellow too
Singing and dancing right with you

Altogether now, altogether
Play with the music
Play with the sound
Keep those feet planted on the ground

Richer deeper, fuller sound
Round and round and round we go
Round and round and round we go

Let it flow, within me, within me
To set me free
Of all this pain and agony

TRAVELLER by Laara Chantel

"About 9 years ago, I was given a gift to participate in Edwin and Cheryl's week long intensive in magnificent Tofino. Singing was a huge dormant passion I had allowed to waste since I was very young, and I knew all my life the passion within me to touch other 's hearts through sound. Life has its way of showing up with other things to attend to. I had given my power away... How long... Lifetimes including this one until I was very done, and asking, asking.. trying., Being.., and Real People Music came along. The unfolding of what was truly within through the archetypes was a huge shift in my life, the stories we all wrote through tears, and rage, and humour to our own selves, to our inner child waiting for how long for us to wake up. I wrote this song, with deep compassion for my Being, and Edwin put the music to it."

TRAVELLER

Quiet voice stirs inside me, I'm a traveller in this unknown land
Quiet voice stirs inside me, I'm a traveller in this unknown land
Quiet voice stirs inside me, I'm a traveller in this known land..

I'm a traveller in this unknown land
Feeling caressed, so loved by the sound of the waves
They're taking me home, I just have to wait
So much beauty yet to explore
I'm a little anxious, searching in this way

Time has gone around, in circles for so long
Searching for some thing outside of me
I feel so soothed, so loved in this state
I'm a traveller in this unknown land

Breezes softly caress my cheeks
I'm meeting new faces, are they just old friends
They're travelling to this unknown land
This land of power and beauty is beckoning me

Time has gone around, in circles for so long
Searching for something outside of me
I feel so soothed, so loved in this state
I'm a traveller in this unknown land

Quiet voice stirs inside me, I'm a traveller in this unknown land
Quiet voice stirs inside me, I'm a traveller in this unknown land
Quiet voice stirs inside me, I'm a traveller in this unknown land.

THE CURTAINS BILLOW IN THE BREEZE–

by Lorna Hannah, B. Ed, CSB, Somatic Sex Educator

"Awareness of what you're actually experiencing—not an idealized notion of perfection—is the essence of all bodily enjoyment." ~ Jack Morin

"This song was pivotal and monumental for me. With the writing and singing of 'The Curtains Billow in the Breeze', I came to realize that I, as a woman, can own my eroticism and my sexual desires and can assertively and actively express them in ways that are powerful and powerfully erotic for me, and that I can be with a man who thrives on my living fully, which further supports me in opening even more to the sexual, erotic realms of my experience. The song is sung quite slowly and sensually, drawing out each stanza like enjoying slow, deeply intimate and enriching sex. I've enjoyed thinking about the various ways this song could be sung to represent the full spectrum of how I can express myself erotically!

The song was originally called A Queendom to Rule as it was the Queen, in her Sovereignty, who claimed her erotic nature, expressing it with her male Lover, with references to them sitting on their thrones. This was a very emotionally wrenching song to sing initially as I realized and embodied this fresh way of seeing.... an awakening of sorts that I truly can own and express my erotic and sexual desires. For weeks after this Sovereign Singing course, I sang the song, over and over, embodying its truth more and more each time, feeling where it was in my body each time. Two months after this song was written, I sang it again at the next Sovereign Singing course, and it was a whole different experience; the truth was embodied! I am now living this song in my 'real' life."

THE CURTAINS BILLOW IN THE BREEZE

The curtains billow in the breeze
Reflecting light of moon
My body glistens in the glow
With sweat upon my breast

You sit so tall upon your throne
Your eager body bared for me
Your rod of life arises strong
With every step I take

I now stand very near,
I'm just beyond your grasp
I look upon your hungry gaze
And see the love that we shall eat

I take your fingers, taste them sweet
Then loose your hands to let them roam
And while you feel my land and sea
I firmly stroke your staff of man

The earth begins to tremble
The lava starts to rise
I move my hips to find my home
Upon my throne of you

Ah ah ah, ah ah ah ah, ah ah ah ah ah ah ah
And now that we are both
Sitting on our thrones
We will fuck the whole night through

Ah ah ah, ah ah ah ah ah ah
We'll make love the whole night long

Ah ah ah, aha…

LITTLE CHILD by Jennifer Stackpole

'Little Child' is a song that truly changed my life. When I was four weeks old, my paediatrician discovered that I had a very serious heart murmur. For the first four years of my life, it was touch and go. I was sick often and my parents didn't know whether or not I was going to make it.

Eventually, the doctor told my mom that I grew out of my heart murmur. However, life was still not easy. From a very early age, I believed that, because I had been so sick and because I was born 'imperfect', I was somehow 'damaged.' Once my heart murmur was detected, my father withdrew more and more. He couldn't handle seeing me sick. It was as if he thought he had, somehow, done something to cause it. As a result, I grew up thinking I caused him to withdraw.

Long story short, when I went to my first Tofino I had no idea how much my heart was still hurting - until I discovered what condition my Lovers were in. I had a lot of healing yet to do and I wasn't even aware of it up until that point. I spent a lot of time working with my Lovers and 'Little Child' was the result of that. That song was my way of going back to my infant self. Through that song, I was able to tell that precious baby girl that she really was fine all along, that she wasn't 'damaged', that she was loved and that she would grow up to change the world in her own special way. 'Little Child' was a love song to my inner child, in a way, and it healed me from so many of the hurts I had experienced growing up.

I'm grateful for that song in a way I can't express. It was the first time I truly expressed what was in my heart - without censoring it or worrying about what anyone else would think about it (or me). I had been writing and recording my own songs for 3 years before I wrote 'Little Child,' but that song freed me from my self-imposed prison of self-judgment and criticism. I haven't been the same since and I'm more grateful for that than I know how to express.

Little Child

Little child
such a little child
such a blessed little perfect baby girl
little child
little child
what a sacred holy little perfect little child

you'll grow up to be brave
you'll grow up to be strong
you'll grow up to be loving and adored
you'll grow up to be free from the pain that you see
and you'll help to heal your soul

little girl
such a little girl
such a healthy loving strong baby girl
baby girl
you are loved
and you're perfect as you are

you've grown up to be brave
you've grown up to be strong
you've grown up to be loving and adored
you've grown up to be free
from the pain that you see
and you've helped to heal the world

you've grown up to be brave
you've grown up to be strong
you've grown up to be loving and adored
you've grown up to be free
from the pain that you see
and you've helped to heal the world

little child
such a little child
such a blessed little perfect baby girl
little child
you are loved
you're perfect as you are

you've grown up to be brave
you've grown up to be strong
you've grown up to be loving and adored
you've grown up to be free
from the pain that you see
and you've helped to heal the world

Music is Love - and Love is all there is

LOVE IS LIKE THE OCEAN by Ellie S

"I felt compelled to go to Tofino for the first time and attend Edwin Coppard's workshop 'Your Voice is the Messenger of Your Soul'. I was quite nervous as I usually get shy about singing in public. However, my dream is to facilitate a non-traditional children's/ youth choir. Thus I attended Edwin's workshop.

After a couple of exercises, I felt very frustrated and at one point, very angry. Angry that I wasn't getting it; i.e., the exercise. It seemed like everyone did and I didn't. I think it basically was writing words to a song. The words just didn't seem to flow as seems too often happen when I try to 'force' words onto a page, or so it seems.

As I didn't come up with a song, I left the room and went to walk along the beach. I was ready to literally self-baptize myself in a sense, clearing and cleansing myself of my anger by stepping right into the ocean. If I had a towel and a change of clothes with me, I would have walked right into the ocean, despite the coldness. I was that angry and determined, at the time! It was while I was standing facing the ocean, that the words came to me:

LOVE IS LIKE THE OCEAN

Love is like the ocean,
Love is like the ocean,
Its wa-a-a-aves keep a rolling

Love is like a forest
Love is like a forest
It i-i-i-is protective

Love is like a mountain
Love is like a mountain
So hi-i-i-gh

Love is in the air
Love is in the air
It i-i-i-is everywhere.

I really FELT and experienced that song deep within me. I truly resonated with it and connected with it deeply. It helped me to dissolve the anger that I felt within me. I came to leaving a lot calmer and more peaceful within myself than when I arrived."

LIFE'S BIG STAGE by Nolin Maurier

"Once married, my wife and I had expressed the desire to have a baby. When I arrived in Tofino, I had no idea I would create a song for the son we never had at the time. We did an event where we were aligning our archetypes on the beach, and with the help of Edwin's son Ulysses and others we created the spiritual movement of my son to be. Without getting into the details of the event, I must say it was one of the most emotional and amazing experiences of my life (aside from the real birth of my son!). It felt so real that I was truly meant to have a child, and I really trusted this would come true in my life. During the course of the event this song started to take on a path of its own, and I realized what I was creating was a lullaby or something like that for my child. With Edwin's help we were able to put the song together with music, and from there I spent time after the event to work further on the song, until I felt it was complete. We had some complications having a child with two miscarriages, one that was four months in, but we did end up eventually having a healthy baby boy! We named our child Sage, and we are so very happy with our new addition. I treasure my new life, and I also treasured my experiences in Tofino with Edwin. It may be hard to 'get' the song unless it is played with music, and maybe someday you will hear this song yourself."

LIFE'S BIG STAGE

Sage, Sage in the corner of my heart - At the peak of the flow - You never let go

The love that we have - You were so far - And now you are here - Born from tears

Curled up with innocence - And I get a sense - That you'll be the sage of our hearts

CHORUS

Sage, Sage you are my gauge - release this rage upon life's big stage

Sage, Sage you are my gauge - release this rage upon life's big stage

I hold you so close - The wife of my life - Never let go - Die in my arms

The one that is ours - The peak of the ocean - The waves of our dreams - Come my love

Born from the sun - Whoever you are - I will always love

CHORUS

Sage, Sage you are my gauge - release this cage upon life's big stage

Sage, Sage you are my gauge - release this cage upon life's big stage

The love that you bring - The joy that you sing - Something I'll treasure for long

It's truly for us - And that is the Sage - That is in all of us

CHORUS

Sage, Sage you are my gauge - turn this page upon life's big stage

Sage, Sage you are my gauge - turn this page upon life's big stage

Hang on the ride - And not too tight - Keep it just right - Never too loose

I free you now child - So you can go free - Together with mom and me…

CHORUS

Sage, Sage you are my gauge - release this rage upon life's big stage

Sage, Sage you are my gauge - release this cage upon life's big stage

Sage, Sage you are my gauge - turn this page upon life's big stage

COLD by Cheryl Coppard

"In the early days of exploring our song writing process, we were holding a weekend course at our house. As soon as we started the song writing process, I felt this dull pain inside. I started writing, searching deeply for the language that would express the particular flavour of what I was feeling. As I progressed through writing the song, a memory came up. When I was around 3 years old I became acquainted with a girl who would be my best friend through childhood. We spent so much time together in all those years. Then suddenly everything changed when I was 13. After returning from a summer vacation with my family and seeing her ahead on the street on the first day of school, I ran to catch up with her, eager to see her. But she crossed the street again and again to avoid me. Apparently our friendship had ended without any clue, without any explanation. I told no one. I think I must have been in shock and numb at the time. Writing and singing this song allowed me to feel and express the deep pain, despair and aloneness I was still holding inside after all those years."

COLD

Octopus undulating under a frozen lake
A freak of nature, a wretched mistake
Somewhere in the north
Aurora Borealis freezes into eyes of blue

Fissures and rainbows remain all year long
Fracture the ice with a silent moan
Into twin thoughts of sapphire stone
Wear them on your fingers
Cold rays of being alone

Go away now, Go away home
Silver shadow 'round the telephone
Climb up your mind
Climb up to find
The stickleback trout that lives there alone
All alone

When Childhood Dies – by Elliot Willis

"Tofino is a place I deeply love, with its Pacific Ocean stretching all the way to China. The battering of wind and waves are written in twisted tree growth, smooth rocks and hidden sea caves. What a fabulous place for the profound process of Sovereign Voice.

On day four I felt good again after my massive cleansing induced by our Lover archetype work the day before. I never knew how much my inner Lovers were dominated by my childhood relationship with my older brother, a gorgeous, overly critical, highly articulate lad. I sat down on the deck in the sun fresh air with the sound of the waves below and put pen to paper for a Sovereign archetype song, when a 13 yr. old young man in our group ran up and announced 'There's a dead deer on the beach!"

As I wondered what would I do with this information out came these lyrics, which with their melody form my new Sovereign perspective on my old buried pain of coming into life as a youngster, loving and looking up to someone who professed to really hate me.

Singing this song for our group and writing it now brings me to tears - both for my own healing, knowing how many ways I have striven in vain to be "good enough" in my life, and knowing one person in our circle shared, as we supported her, that she was recently enduring torment from an immature adult brother. I see both of us strong and at peace in our own Sovereign power."

When Childhood Dies

When childhood dies the nightmares are all over, and all the lies are proven wrong,
Sun illuminates my darkest sores, shining light on treasures there.

In the hollowed places of my soul, where I bravely stood the tide,
And my weaknesses wash out of me, leaving only strength behind.

I can cherish every shining stone, every fragile seashell hurled,
By the pounding of the ocean waves, softened walls where water curled.

Rise the King from serving endlessly; seat the Queen from darkness deep,
Cast old bodies on my wave wept shore, I take my new Sovereign seat.

NOTHING - by Arlaine Johansen

"When I wrote this I thought it was just a little nothing sort of light song, and then, afterwards, when I got down to feel it and sing it I started to cry. I am not a crying person really. So when buckets just released from my eyes I was shocked. Tears were literally pouring out of me like a button had been pressed that had never been pressed before, and that I had needed to press it. At the time, I was in a relationship where there was a lot of adversity that I had thought were single events. It turns out they weren't. It was a stream of conflict that I could not resolve as it turned out not to be from me. I had tuned out most feeling as it was too painful to keep hoping for resolution and that sweet, absolute love you get with respect/trust and deeper layers of connection.

For me this song opened a door that allowed me to recognize and heal a part of myself that I had forgotten and purposely pushed aside for at least 3 years."

NOTHING

What's it like to feel nothing?

Not the sun or wind's bite
Warm grass tight
Beneath my feet.
I won't ever know what that's like
The rock talks and say it's nice.
The trees brag about the shade
How peaceful a place they made.

What's it like to feel nothing?

I can't imagine such torment
Not to feel each message sent.
Soft glances, tenderness, just enhances
Why is it that there is a lack
Of people reaching forward instead of back?
Is this all hidden too deeply,
For each and everyone not to sleep
Through the waking hours as well?

Who wants to feel nothing?

CONSECRATION by James MacFarlane

"At a Tofino workshop, it was Edwin who introduced me to the concept of the primary archetypes that we all interact with in our psyche. It was a metamorphosis for me, an awakening of a new and dynamic way of understanding myself and appreciating myself. It provided me with a real tool to better understand my emotions, to control my emotions to outside stimuli, and to better orchestrate the force of each archetype that dances freely within our unique personalities.

Coming to understand for the first time how we are a balance of Warrior, Magician, Lover and Sovereign was incredibly exciting for me. Knowledge is a powerful thing and when I came to know that my own happiness and wellbeing was greatly reliant on which particular archetypal force was dominant in my interpersonal interactions with others, it provided me with an authentic frame of reference to live my life in a more fulfilled and considerate manner. Both to myself and to all others who I come across along the path of life. It is our shared human experience.

Within the archetype exercises in Tofino the concept of a male and female side within us was introduced. At first I was skeptical, never before having ventured out without my male dominant perspective. However I came to realize that we are in reality a mixture of male and female genealogy and by a force of nature we are the result of male and female coming together and therefore we have male and female genes coursing through our bodies, our minds and for that matter our souls. It is an enormous concept to comprehend at a very mature stage in life.

A simple example of this reality is the futility and misconception of the old saying that "men don't cry, only women cry." The truth is that both men and women cry and we do so because as humans we share male and female tendencies within our being. It is said women are weaker than men, which is also not true as women are much stronger than men in many instances (the ferocity of a mother protecting her children is renowned). Of course we know that men and women take on different roles in the living of life (nurturing children for example), yet within the boundaries of our own unique being we house both female and male aspects of personality and functionality.

Prior to Christopher Columbus venturing out beyond the known horizon, people believed the world was flat. The archetype work with Edwin in Tofino was my own personal discovery that the world is round not flat. Inspired by this new and exciting knowledge I wrote this song dedicated to the archetypes that inhabit our bodies, minds and souls.

It is interesting that I first find the melody and I develop both the melody and the words simultaneously. The melody came from a medieval Gothic tone that was resonating in my mind. For this particular song I had a very strong sense of my own heritage stretching back to the turbulent times of the Middle Ages in Scotland. It was after my first introduction to archetype work with Edwin in Tofino. I clearly could see and appreciate that the sinews of my own mind and body stretched very far back to my ancestors who had endured the vagaries of life and survived somehow, and as a result I am able to enjoy the wonderful gift of life in this present time. I was thankful to all of the mothers from time immemorial who had borne a child, and the fathers that supported them, that I could be born and enjoy all that life is and can be.

It is a song that consecrates the combined male and female energy, the interplay of Warrior, Magician, Lover and Sovereign that found it's resting place in my mind, body and spirit. Consecration is the act of blessing, making holy, taking something considered ordinary and making it revered and sacred. So this song to the archetypes is a new and dynamic way for me, through this song of Consecration, to bring blessing to the gift of life in all its dynamic wonder. The words and the melody highlight the sacred nature of our being and celebrate the gift of life we all enjoy. Encouraging us to live life to the full with a better understanding of who we are and what we can be, as well as being mindful and considerate about what we pass along to future generations. My song of consecration is a prayer of thanks and praise for the blessed state of being we have been given to enjoy and make much of and understand better in ourselves and in the being of our fellow travellers who journey with us."

CONSECRATION

On consecrated ground, confer ritual cleansing
Washed pure in holy water, hear Angelic praising
Summon the Priests, time for sacred blessing
Crowned with gold, affirmed in full regal bearing

My Queen for life, the summit of my desire
Let not feast or famine, quench our inner fire
Let the Minstrels prance, with lute and lyre
To our Jesters, waken up our cosmic choir

Far to the horizon, our Kingdom reigns
Legions of Horsemen gallop without restrain
Night and Day, a vigilant watch maintains
Day and Night, protecting our sovereign peace
No taming their aim

Plagued by affection, our hearts never stray
Abundant our pleasures, all senses at play
Earth tasting Heaven, love has its soulful say
Gracing the flesh, adjoined we devoutly pray

About The Authors

Edwin Coppard

Anyone who has come to any of Edwin's events knows there is no one like Edwin anywhere! He has always walked his own path far away from the musical conventions of society. Over the past 25 years he has followed this road less travelled and rediscovered the principles and power of sound and song. From his out-of-the-box premise that anyone can sing he has developed **'Sovereign Singing'**, the modern miracle of voice development.

International teacher and performer, he has appeared live in front of huge audiences and repeatedly astounded them with the speed and magic of watching someone's voice change within seconds and minutes. Everywhere he goes all over the world, he blows people away with his demonstrations. He opens people's minds to the potential of music in their own lives and music's potential to bring everyone together.

Leading international speakers use Edwin to augment their events, including Tony Robbins, Mark Victor Hansen, James Skinner and T. Harv Eker. Companies large and small use Edwin to bring life and energy to the work place, to enliven creativity, to awaken natural teamwork, and to bring fun and mutual appreciation to everyone.

With up to 40 nations represented at some of the events, Edwin proves that music is the universal language through which all people can communicate by getting everyone singing together in minutes.

Edwin has been deeply involved in music all his life. As a young boy in a choir school in England he sang Gregorian chants. In Canada as young man in high school he belonged to the Shockers, a band that became very well known, winning the PNE Battle of the Bands, playing on national TV, and opening for such acts as Billy Preston and the Everly Brothers. When the band broke up, Edwin created a solo career out of which came the album 'Dawning Day,' and several hit singles in Canada, including 'Come and See My Man, ' which made the billboard top 10.

Edwin has always been a singer, but he began to be curious about the voice – why it would be dependable one day and not the next. It was this curiosity that led him in 1982 to the innovative opera-trained teacher Trudy Buckler, who opened his eyes to the physicality of sound production. After studying with her for some time he began to teach his own personal clients.

Edwin also studied Kinesiology through Brain Gym creator Paul Dennison. Integrating Kinesiology with his new teaching techniques created even more amazing results. It was around this time, in 1986, that Edwin realized he could teach anyone to sing.

Edwin created seminars based on his new processes. In 1989 he met Tony Robbins. Tony was so impressed with Edwin's abilities, he asked Edwin to teach at his first Life Mastery Course. Edwin continues to teach at all Anthony Robin's Life Mastery Courses. He also works with Tony's Exclusive Platinum Group.

"*Because singing brings everyone together, makes them HAPPIER, & generates ENERGY. Edwin is THE BEST IN THE WORLD at getting people to sing INSTANTLY naturally.*" - Anthony Robbins

In 1991 Edwin was introduced to a fascinating Archetype Theory, and subsequently developed a profound process. With this remaining piece Edwin, with his wife Cheryl, created **'Sovereign Singing'** and inaugurated **'Your Voice Is The Messenger of Your Soul'**, a flagship six-day event in Tofino, BC. This world class intensive is regarded as one of the most life changing experiences offered anywhere in the world.

Real People Music is the culmination of 30+ years of experience. The uniqueness of Edwin's approach has touched tens of thousands of people, changing voices and lives. Edwin continues to travel the globe and teach, and is creating a training course to empower others to share the gift of music with the world. Edwin currently lives in Victoria, BC, Canada, with his wife and 2 sons.

Cheryl Coppard, BFA

Cheryl Coppard was born in British Columbia, Canada. Both her parents are musical; however, it was her father who was particularly fond of the accordion! She started young, taking lessons, competing and teaching the accordion until she was 17. She feels very grateful for that gift of music, grateful to have a way to express that which can't be put into words.

Cheryl is also a visual artist, graduating with a BFA cum laude from Maharishi University of Management, a wonderful university in Iowa, USA, which has at its basis the development of consciousness.

Cheryl and Edwin married in 1987 and since then she has been involved in developing all the programs of Real People Music. Her particular expertise is in the area of the Four Living Archetypes. She gives private and group sessions, guiding people to discover this extraordinary landscape inside. She guides people through an interactive process whereby they can explore this inner world and resolve specific issues using the Living Archetypes. For Cheryl, being able to utilize the inner world of the Four Archetypes is an essential skill we all need to understand ourselves and to be able to gracefully and easily affect transformation from the inside out.

Cheryl and Edwin have two sons, Ulysses and Zane, who are talented musicians in their own right.

Success Resources

We at Real People Music are pleased to offer a series of learning experiences on your journey to find your Unbounded Voice and your inner world of the Living Archetypes.

All our seminars include key principles that we keep building upon in longer events.

Wake Up and Sing!
Our 1 - Day Event!

A special 'Wild Voice Workout' to reconnect the voice to the body:

- Unlock energy that lasts all day! Impact your presence when giving presentations! Become more balanced, relaxed and focused!
- Shatter the current boundaries of your voice!
- Become more flexible, no matter what your current state of health!
- Breathe freely!
- Learn to Jam together and create music from deep connection with others!

Introduction to the field of unbounded emotional energy and the Unbounded Voice:

- Be awestruck by the new power in your voice!
- Be amazed by your new musicality!
- Feel what it's like to finally, truly, express your emotions

Our unique approach to song writing:

- Learn to access your physical body memory and unlock unbounded creativity!

- Learn to write songs that will heal your life and impact your surroundings!
- Gain inspiration and insights that will move you forward and manifest what you need!

An introduction to your Living Archetypes:

- Learn how to find and communicate with your Living Archetypes!
- Open up this world of insight, inspiration and revelation!
- Be amazed when you realize the basis of your strengths and weaknesses!
- Begin the healing process inside!

A celebration of sound and song:

- The power of sharing the truth inside you is amazing for your own growth and confidence, and for the realization of the impact you can have on others!
- This experience is a blast!
- Everyone shares their songs with others!
- It's a celebration of our lives and stories, and a truly connecting experience!

Wild Voice Extravaganza
Our 3 - Day Event!

It is recommended to have either experienced the 1-Day 'Wake Up and Sing' event, participated in our on-line training, taken Real People Music sessions, or seen Edwin at a live event before taking the Wild Voice Extravaganza 3-Day!

Strengthening the 'Wild Voice Workout' from the 1 - Day Wake Up and Sing event!

For increased impact and effect, we will be adding:

- The mastering of a new model of projection to connect with the whole room.
- How to use the sound of your voice to heal your body and impact others.
- Learn to 'ride the waves' of audience emotion to create powerful empathy and impact.
- Learn more whole brain integration techniques to improve the quality of your life.
- More individual attention and demonstrations.

Reinforcing your connection with the field of unbounded emotional energy, with the Unbounded Voice

The Art of Song writing:

- Write more songs!

- Learn to write songs with a specific focus. Be amazed at the flow of originality!
- Learn to write songs to resolve challenges in business, relationships, health, etc.
- Learn to write songs that manifest.

Deepening the Journey of the Living Archetypes:

- Discover, explore and integrate the Male and Female Archetypes to understand yourself and others!
- Create individual rituals of dance and song to awaken the empowering qualities of each Living Archetype!
- Learn how to access qualities you will need to achieve maximum results!
- Integrate all the Living Archetypes as a team!
- How to live in 'The Zone' of peak performance!
- Learn how to use this Ultimate Board of Directors to guide your life.

Celebration of Sound and Song:

- Every night we share our songs to practice becoming great performers and presenters!
- We learn to celebrate life, enjoy each other, support each other, and experience community building in a new way.
- There will be a CD/DVD of the final evening for each participant.
- At our final concert, we will sing a song together that we have written together to manifest something powerful for our world!

Your Voice is the Messenger of Your Soul

Our 6 - Day Event

Our flagship event!

Begin to live your life in Sovereignty!

Only 16 people, by application, can attend this event!

This course is a prerequisite for our teacher training programs starting in 2013.

The group will create a CD/DVD of their songs and live performances that they share during the week.

Personal Sessions, business consultations, music production, and custom seminars are available with Edwin and/or Cheryl.

Check out our website: www.realpeoplemusic.com

Printed in Australia
AUOC011134221112
254480AU00001BA/1/P

9 781922 118080